Textbooks in School and Society

The Garland Bibliographies
in Contemporary Education
(Advisory Editor Joseph M. McCarthy)
Vol. 6

Garland Reference Library
of the Social Sciences
Vol. 405

THE GARLAND BIBLIOGRAPHIES IN CONTEMPORARY EDUCATION

Advisory Editor:
Joseph M. McCarthy

Textbooks in School and Society

*An Annotated Bibliography
and Guide to Research*

Arthur Woodward
David L. Elliott
Kathleen Carter Nagel

GARLAND PUBLISHING, INC., · NEW YORK & LONDON
1988

Library of Congress Cataloging-in-Publication Data

Woodward, Arthur, 1950–
  Textbooks in school and society : an annotated bibliography and
guide to research / Arthur Woodward, David L. Elliot, Kathleen
Carter Nagel.
    p.   cm.—(The Garland bibliographies in contemporary
education ; vol. 6) (Garland reference library of the social
sciences : vol. 405)
  Includes index.
  ISBN 0-8240-8390-3 (alk. paper)
  1. Textbooks—United States—Bibliography. I. Elliot, David L.,
1929– . II. Nagel, Kathleen Carter. III. Title. IV. Series:
Garland bibliographies in contemporary education ; v. 6. V. Series:
Garland reference library of social science ; v. 405.
Z5817.W64   1988
[LB3047]
016.37—dc19   87-35302
                                                       CIP

Printed on acid-free, 250-year-life paper
Manufactured in the United States of America

CONTENTS

Introduction
1. The Textbook as an Object of Research.
2. Structure of the Bibliography.
   a) Subject and Scope.
   b) Sources of References.
3. Overview of Bibliographic Topics.

TEXTBOOK PRODUCERS AND CONSUMERS

EVALUATION AND CRITICISM OF TEXTBOOKS

Introduction

1. THE TEXTBOOK AS AN OBJECT OF RESEARCH

Textbooks have been standard schoolroom fixtures for as long as most living citizens of this country can remember. Many turn-of-the-century students were introduced to reading through the moralistic McGuffey Readers and struggled through the rather drab and colorless pages of volumes on history, geography and civics. In contrast, today's textbooks contain not only narrative content accompanied by colorful photographs and graphics, but also section and chapter exercises that are extended through the use of worksheets and other materials. Moreover, the textbook and its related student materials are packaged together with teacher's editions and tests in grade-level sets that amount to content area programs rather than mere texts.

Textbooks are important and intriguing artifacts of a literate, industrial society. On the one hand, they reflect a kind of national consensus regarding the knowledge and values that members of the society want transmitted to their children; on the other hand, textbooks incorporate much of current thought concerning the psychology of learning and the implications of that thought for pedagogy. Significantly, in the last several decades, textbooks have taken over the curriculum in many schools of this nation, particularly at the elementary and junior high levels. Teachers rely on textbook programs to supply not only subject matter content, but also teaching strategies and tactics in the form of elaborately worked out approaches to the presentation of the major school subjects and detailed lesson plans. Local curriculum development has been largely replaced by the work of authors, publishers, and textbook selection committees.

The Unstudied Curriculum Component

In view of its significant role in American elementary and secondary education, it is astonishing to discover that the textbook has not been studied by educational researchers for much longer than the past ten years. The research on teaching and learning that took place from the 1950s through

1

most of the 1970s included classroom studies of teaching and
alternative approaches to instruction in the basic subject
areas and school-based studies of innovation and change in the
curriculum. However, in virtually all of these the textbook
was unacknowledged as a possible variable; instead, it was
treated like part of the classroom furniture, a given that did
not significantly influence teaching and learning one way or
the other.

Indeed, while recent studies indicate that schooling in
the 20th century is characterized by a heavy and pervasive dependence on textbooks, research and commentary has been spo-
radic and faddish, being marked by peaks of brief interest
followed by valleys of neglect. The 30th yearbook of the
National Society for the Study of Education, published in 1931
(Item 201) and Lee Cronbach's edited volume, Text Materials in
Modern Education, published in 1955 (Item 179) represent two
such peaks; both were followed by two decades of silence.

During the last two decades, published critiques of textbooks have tended to focus on single issues or problems. For
example, although we have included in this volume only the
most significant and interesting items on the representation
of ethnic minorities and women in textbooks, literally hundreds of such articles have appeared. Censorship and the
treatment of controversial issues have also been persistent
themes in recent decades. In addition, there have been numerous "one-shot" articles on such topics as the treatment of
specific immigrant groups or American Indians in social studies books, aging or environmental issues in biology texts, and
the Great Depression or the Cold War in high school U.S. history volumes. Prior to the 1970s, however, there was virtually no attention given to wider issues pertaining to the curriculum role and the quality and instructional design of textbooks.

Recognition At Last

The last few years has seen a marked change in the nature
and scope of research and commentary on textbooks. Prompted
primarily by the report of the National Commission on Excellence in Education (016), researchers and critics have recognized textbooks as important elements in any attempt to improve the quality of education and, as such, an important topic for research and criticism. In contrast to previous periods, this more recent research has been broadly based and

cumulative and, signficantly, a cadre of scholars has emerged
that has devoted much time to researching particular problems
and issues related to textbooks and the curriculum. Apparent-
ly, the textbook has become a respectable and interesting object for scholarly study and, as each new article is published, additional interest and research is generated.

Also notable is the interdisciplinary nature of much of
the recently published work on textbooks. While research in
this volume does include articles on narrow topics such as the
instructional use of photographs, other topics, such as the
effect of state policies on the selection of textbooks, must
of necessity draw upon research in other areas. Thus, discussions of readability often refer to school district selection
policy issues as, for example, whether readability formulas
should be used as a way of judging the suitability of textbooks for particular schools and students. Similarly, a discussion of state adoption of textbooks inevitably involves
topics such as the problem of "mentioning" (i.e., the breadth,
as opposed to depth, of topic coverage), pressures from special interest groups concerning controversial content, or the
development of "national" textbooks that reflect some sort of
"market consensus" on the curriculum.

In the future, more and more scholarship should focus on
the relationships among the many problems and issues that are
presented by the examination of textbooks in relation to the
overall enterprise of American education. At present, however, there are still areas in which the published articles
and monographs are treated in isolation. For example, as we
report in more detail below, articles dealing with controversial issues and censorship typically either report incidents
of censorship or take the position that censorship is inher-
ently bad and in violation of the First Amendment and/or professional prerogative, whatever the situation. Little attempt
is made to relate censorship to the complex policy, philosophical, and psychological issues that surround it as a topic.

2. STRUCTURE OF THE BIBLIOGRAPHY

Subject and Scope.

This bibliography encompasses research and critical commentary on selected aspects of school textbooks and their relationship to teaching and learning and to educational policy-making in school programs at the elementary and secondary levels. Issues and problems pertaining to such matters as instructional design, content coverage and accuracy, selection standards and procedures, the influence of major adoption states, and censorship have been discussed increasingly in the literature over the past two or three decades.

This annotated bibliography is intended to provide a comprehensive, up-to-date reference work for researchers and educators interested in the most significant contributions that have been made to our knowledge about textbooks, how they are produced and selected, and how they function in the schools. In the development of this bibliography, we attempted to include only the most significant and important works in thoroughly researched areas (e.g., the representation of women and ethnic minority groups), while at the same time indicating those areas that have not yet been adequately studied. Most of the items deal with textbooks in the United States; non-English works have not been included. Most of the authors whose works have been included are professional educators and educational researchers; however, significant works by laypeople (e.g., Frances Fitzgerald) have also been included.

Although journal and book titles on textbooks can be traced back to the late 1800s, we concentrated on finding book-length studies, monographs, and journal articles published since 1975 and included only those earlier items that we thought made a lasting contribution to our knowledge of the area. Perhaps not surprisingly, the concerns of over 30 years ago were very similar to the ones currently at issue. The inclusion of "historical" research items (limited in number though they are) is, we feel, a major contribution of this book. For if researchers fail to ground their work and think-

5

ing in the work of those that preceded them, then current efforts are inevitably repetitive and (often) uninformed. A
historical perspective has important implications for research
and discussion on textbook policy and curriculum issues. Indeed, as we suggest below, research published as early as the
turn of the century (and not well-known until now) shows that
teacher dependence on textbook was widespread and a problem of
great concern.

Sources of References

A number of standard references were consulted in compil-
ing this bibliography. Among these were the Education Index,
the ERIC Resources in Education and Current Index to Journals
in Education, Dissertation Abstracts, Cumulative Book Index,
the Library of Congress Subject Catalog, Encyclopedia of Educational Research, Review of Educational Research, Review of
Research in Education, Encyclopedia of Education, and the
Handbook of Research in Teaching. We also discovered a number
of important articles through happenstance and serendipity.
For example, it was only by chance that we discovered a special issue of Phi Delta Kappan devoted to textbooks (see Item
G021). The articles in this issue, like some of the others we
came across, provided an interesting commentary on the issues
related to textbook quality that were important to contemporary critics and researchers.

The sources of the items included in this bibliography
cover a wide range. Much of the research reported, such as
studies of text readability, "considerate" text, and reading
comprehension, comes out of psychology and other social science disciplines and is reported in scholarly journals. However, the majority of the articles appear in professionl journals and magazines, including those published for lawyers,
home economists, and policy makers as well as teachers and
other professional educators. While some of the journals and
magazines employed single topics as issue themes (as, for example, the School Library Journal reporting regularly on censorship), most included articles on a wide range of topics in
each issue, occasionally including one or two on textbooks.

3. OVERVIEW OF BIBLIOGRAPHIC TOPICS

Textbooks Producers and Consumers

Textbook Use and Curriculum Role. In the last few years, school reform has had two main thrusts: the first has been to increase the level of student achievement and to strengthen the school curriculum; the second consists of reforms leading to the "professionalization" of teaching. Both of these thrusts are related to textbooks: students read textbook chapters and complete assignments, and teachers rely on textbooks to provide instruction through narrative and exercises as well as through teacher's edition lesson plans and classroom activities.

If students and teachers depend on textbooks, then the quality of textbooks and accompanying materials directly affects the quality of teaching and learning in school classrooms. Thus, if textbooks "mention" numerous topics, but treat none in depth, or if teacher's guides provide detailed prescriptions for basic skill practice but little for critical thinking, then textbooks become an important element in educational reform.

To what extent are textbooks used in schools and to what extent are teachers dependent upon them and their accompanying teacher's guides? A number of systematic research reports have substantiated anecdotal reportage that textbooks do, indeed, play a crucial part in school programs. Both historical reports (from the beginning of the century) and more recent research indicate that from 75% to 90% of classroom instructional time is structured by textbook programs. Given this heavy dependence, the instructional quality of these materials becomes an important consideration in efforts to reform the curriculum.

Teacher's guides, as central components of multi-level textbook programs, are of particular concern. A number of articles examine the nature of these guides and the "technology" of instruction in recently published basal reading ser-

ies. This research seems to indicate that teacher's guides
have become increasingly prescriptive and leave less and less
room for independent teacher decision making. In addition,
the designs of basal series for reading and other subjects include strict sequencing prescriptions and testing and manage-
ment systems that essentially force the teacher to follow a
pre-ordained instructional plan. Little leeway is given for
teachers to change the sequence of topics or to add or delete
topics.

If teachers and students did not use textbooks as slav-
ishly as they appear to, there would be less concern about improving the quality of textbooks. Indeed, as part of a larger
group of resources to be drawn upon when appropriate, the net
effect of textbooks on educational quality would be lessened
and, concommitantly, the importance of textbooks to the reform
movement would be greatly reduced. But that is not the case
and, as the articles included in this section indicate, the
quality of textbook programs and policies affecting that quality are in need of serious attention.

Textbook Selection. The wide variety of articles in this
section cover a multitude of discrete as well as overlapping
topics with authorship ranging from representatives of state
departments of education to researchers in private institutions. The large number of research articles reflects the
nationwide concern for an organized, defensible textbook selection process. Topics range from discussions of the lack of
uniformity among states in their textbook selection processes,
to the influence of adoption states, to recommended steps to
be taken in making selections.

A number of articles address the acute desire on the part
of school districts to identify or develop a sure-fire approach to selection that can be relied upon to identify textbooks which best fit their needs. These articles variously
identify teachers, administrators, and subject area specialists as playing crucial roles in selection. Also recommended
is the use of skill tracing or categorical questions related
to content, visual appeal, or durability as means to discrimi-
nate among textbooks. Some authors urge school districts to
consider textbooks in light of their own curriculum priorities
while others decry the occasions where the best cost-cutting
deal between district and publishing company, more than any
curriculum considerations, ultimately determines the textbook selected.

In sum, the articles in this section underscore the disparate and often highly unsatisfactory means by which textbooks are selected and the need for more carefully thought out guidance in this area.

The Production and Marketing of Textbooks

The Textbook Industry. By and large, the publishing industry remains a mystery. Little is known publicly about how textbooks are produced, the role of authors, the influence of the market, or the economics of publishing. However, we did find a number of articles and reports that give us at least a glimpse into the industry, but we had to go further afield than the usual professional journals and books to find them. Thus, you will find in this section a number of newspaper and magazine articles because, while there appears to be a reluctance on the part of publishing staffs to write about their own industry, they have been willing to talk to reporters.

At the outset we should mention that we found two types of articles and reports, one laudatory, the other factual and anecdotal. Surprisingly, publishing executives rarely discuss their competition, market share, or the commercial success of various publishing ventures. Not so surprisingly, laudatory articles are usually penned by publishing company executives and cover the common themes of quality, responsiveness, and responsibility. According to these executives, textbooks represent the best that money can buy, reflect current knowledge regarding pedagogy and learning psychology, and incorporate exceptional design quality. Most important, textbook programs reflect what educational consumers want: through networks of salespeople and involvement in professional organizations, publishing companies assess the needs of educators and produce textbooks to fill these needs.

Although relatively little is written about textbook publishing, what is available allows us to make a number of observations about various aspects of the industry. A common theme in the 1930s and recent years has been the issue of copyright dating. In the 1930s, publishers complained about educator demands for recent copyright dates on textbooks they were considering for adoption. The result of this demand, according to reports, was a shorter time cycle in which to prepare new editions of textbooks and hence a poorer quality

product. Similar concern is expressed about the current demand for recent copyright dates. However, whereas publishers
had previously complained about the expectation of a five-year
renewal cycle, now many educators are demanding updates in two
or three years.

Unlike trade publishing where one can be sure that the
author has written the book that bears his or her name, this
is not the case with textbook writing. While data is limited,
concern was expressed as early as the early 1930s about the
practice of using authors only (or mainly) for their scholarly
or professional standing. During that period, the size of the
editorial departments of publishing houses varied, so it seems
clear that some authors were given wide responsibilities and
others were not. Contemporary reports, especially regarding
textbook writing for the elementary grades, paint a picture of
authors who are more valued for their "names," or for their
ability to provide geographic or minority group representation, than for their writing contributions.

Anecdotal reports indicate that those listed as authors
or consultants may comment on chapter outlines and occasionally write sections of the text. However, their major function
seems to be to provide a seal of respectability for the
text. A number of recent reports have alluded to the role of
develoment houses in the design and writing of textbooks, although it is not clear whether these companies have superceded
or merely enhanced in-house editorial departments. What is
clear is that these companies bear much responsibility for
producing textbooks in short time periods. Given the complexity of the materials as well as time pressures, that some publishers rely on development houses is perhaps understandable.
This complexity and time pressure also help to explain the reduced role of authors at the elementary level as compared with
the high school level where authors seem to have a larger
role. Elementary level textbooks are usually multi-level series consisting of numerous components that range from student
texts to teacher's guides, workbooks, and achievement tests
and it is understandable that even three or four co-authors
would be hard pressed to create all these materials.

Relatively little has been written about the changing
nature of the textbook. Research reported in this volume indicates that the page length of textbooks has increased tre-
mendously over the past several decades and that the growing
demand for more colorful and aesthetically pleasing materials

has changed textbooks from black and white volumes of modest size to the weighty and colorful tomes of today. One can speculate that both the length and design qualities of textbooks are a function of "the market" and the changing nature of publishing. Regarding length, the point seems not to be so much that knowledge has increased, necessitating longer books, but that textbooks have become national consensus documents designed to sell in as many communities as possible. The economics of publishing pressures publishers to aim at a national market in order to recoup development and marketing costs. This means that the content of each textbook program must satisfy the curricular demands of states as diverse as California, Texas, and Georgia, and school districts as diverse as Detroit, Scarsdale, and Evanston. Numerous topics must be included in each textbook and, since none can be really well covered, each is simply "mentioned."

Part of the dynamic of the textbook market appears to be consumer demand for textbooks with high quality design characteristics such as four-color illustrations, numerous ancillary materials for students, comprehensive teacher's guides, and recent copyright dates. As the section on textbook selection indicates, these textbook attributes appear to be as, if not more, important than the narrative/conceptual content in determining which textbooks will be purchased. Certainly, the articles on marketing textbooks note the importance of these features in sales appeal.

In keeping with the interest in consumer influence on textbook production, we have also included in this section articles dealing with Learner Verification and Revision (LVR), a procedure that is important in that, if it were implemented, would ensure that textbook passages would be tried out with students and revised prior to publication. On the face of it, this does not seem a very startling idea. (It would be inconceivable for an automobile to be produced without similar input.) However, such is the culture of publishing that, despite a number of state initiatives, LVR has not become a regular part of textbook development.

Ironically, market-driven development costs have made textbook publishing the preserve of a handful of national corporations. Although there are as many as a hundred publishers of school materials, the lion's share of sales goes to about eight companies. As data indicate, these few companies are highly profitable and have been subject to takeovers by con-

glomerates and other publishers. But the cost of retaining a
company's market share and profit margin is careful attention
to what will sell.

Breaking out of the vicious cycle of the market status
quo is the major aim of textbook reformers. However, much
more needs to be known about textbook publishing for, despite
the articles summarized in this volume, publishing remains a
secretive, inaccessible, and mysterious industry.

Innovation and Reform Efforts. The 1960s was the decade
of ambitious curriculum reform efforts. These efforts were
generously supported by federal government grants and many involved the participation of university scholars in the development of non-textbook programs at the elementary level (except for the "new mathematics" texts) and significant re-
development of textbooks at the secondary level. Many of the
results of these projects were known during the late 1960s and
through the 1970s and early 1980s by alphabetical designations
such as ESS, SAPA, SCIS, BSSC Biology, and PSSC Physics in
science and a whole spate of "new social studies" programs,
including Our Working World (OWW), MACOS, DATABANK, and a
number of others at both elementary and secondary levels.

There appears to be little doubt that the participants in
these reform projects believed that they were introducing a
new era of instructional programs in their subject areas.
Content was selected to introduce students to the "structures"
of the scholarly disciplines underlying each subject area and
process (the process of scholarly investigation) was considered to be as important as content (the results of that investigation) that was the traditional textbook fare. Emerging
theory and research in cognitive psychology replaced more established learning theory, major stress was placed on an active role for learners, and such terms as "discovery" and "inquiry" became common parts of educator vocabulary.

However, some not-so-funny things happened on the way to
the classroom, and that is what the selections in this section
are all about. Although there are several studies that survey
three subject areas (mathematics, science and social studies),
most are devoted to describing the "new social studies" programs, how widely they were known and adopted, their effects
on subsequently published textbook programs, and why most are
not around any more. Most of the articles and reports also
focus on teachers and school systems, although there are two

that are concerned with effects on student development (in
science) and attitudes (mathematics).

Although most of the selections in this section are not
about **textbooks** as such, they should be of interest to anyone
who is concerned with either the improvement of textbook programs or in the substitution of more teacher initiative and
the use of a wider variety of instructional resources for the
current dependence on the textbook. If nothing else, the entries in this section are powerful witnesses to the over-
whelming influence of the textbook in American education;
after all, it was confronted with one of the best financed and
comprehensive sets of curriculum reform efforts ever mounted
--and it prevailed.

General Discussion and Special Topics

General References. Ordinarily, a section such as this is
for articles and reports that do not fit elsewhere. However,
it is important to note that, in the present volume, this section includes both recent and historical articles and books
that have had a significant effect in prompting debate about
textbook quality. The work of two authors in particular,
Fitzgerald (346) and Vitz (197), received more public attention, and thus stimulated more general interest in textbooks
than any publication since Flesch's Why Johnny Can't Read
(Item 292).

Fitzgerald's book is written in an eminently readable
style and deals with what everyone has experienced, learning
U.S. history in high school. Fitzgerald argues that the textbooks that are used to teach history have changed from the
colorfully written, exciting volumes written by literate his-
torians in the 1930s and earlier to the dry, sterile "consensus" prose characteristic of the current crop. Undoubtedly,
this book sowed a number of seeds of doubt regarding textbook
quality.

Vitz's widely-cited work has also been important in stim-
ulating interest in textbooks. His analysis of elementary
reading and elementary and secondary social studies textbooks
found that traditional family groups are rarely featured and
that religion has disappeared from accounts of U.S. history
after the period of the American Revolution. These findings
both shocked and surprised many and again focused attention on

textbooks.

The section also includes articles from education encyclo-
pedias and reviews of research that should be of help to those
interested in publications on textbooks, especially those published before 1975 that are not included in this volume. In a
1962 issue of the Review of Educational Research (Item 180),
Davis reviews research reports about textbooks and printed
materials that appeared between 1957 and 1961. In a similar
vein, articles in The International Encyclopedia of Education
Research and Studies (Item 190) and the Encyclopedia of Educational Research (Item 188), provide reviews of research on
topics related to textbooks. Otherwise this section contains
a potpourri of textbook critiques that do not fit in any other
section of this bibliography.

Text Readability. The search for a valid yet easy-to-use
method for matching the difficulty level of textbook prose to
the abilities of students has been going on for a number of
decades. Eight of the articles in this section describe or
criticize well-known readability formulas. Four articles introduce the concept of "considerateness," a relatively new approach to the problem that does not lend itself to word counts
or numerical formulas. Not included in this section is any
discussion of the Degrees of Reading Power (DRP) approach developed by the College Board, although the article by Elliott
and Wiles (Item 214) does describe the use of the Cloze technique with mathematics textbooks.

Treatment of Ethnic Minority Groups and Women. Concern
over the treatment of ethnic minorities was first expressed in
print in a classic study published by the Anti-Defamation
League of B'nai B'rith in 1961 (Item 254), but it was not until a decade later that the force of this concern was strong
enough to have a significant impact on the content of textbooks. During the 1970s, pressures to rid textbooks of the
stereotyping and omission of various groups, including women,
probably had had more effect on the content of American textbooks than any other force in recent years. In California,
for example, textbooks have to measure up to the "legal com-
pliance" provisions of the Education Code, which include
standards for the treatment of women and minority group, or
they cannot even be considered for adoption on other
criteria.

The articles annotated in this section were selected from

a large group of articles on this topic because they describe the findings of systematic research. Most of the articles deal with the portrayal of females and ethnic minority groups, but there are single entries on treatment of the aged and the handicapped.

Subject Matter Content Coverage

The search of titles dealing with subject matter coverage was limited to the five basic school subjects: language arts, mathematics, reading, science, and social studies and we did not include any of the reviews of individual textbooks and textbook programs that appear regularly in some of the journals. The title of this section highlights content because, with rare exception, few of the articles and reports in it deal with other aspects of instructional design such as philosophy and purpose, teaching and learning activities, and provisions for the assessment of student status and achievement. We found no studies describing differences in the ways in which teachers implement textbook programs or of the differential effects of various programs—and varying implementation—on student learning and development.

One main theme that runs through most of the criticisms made across all five subject areas, is that the world as portrayed in textbooks is different in important respects from either the world that is described by the scholar or the "real" world that students experience either directly or indirectly. Those who have studied textbook content have held up a mirror to the instructional programs of the American schools. What we can see in that mirror is highly selective, sanitized, pre-packaged, and often distorted content offered to students in the name of science and social studies and what must seem like endless sequences of isolated skills proffered in the name of reading, writing, and mathematics. We can also see that these programs do, of course, fit in well with the easily administered and easily scored achievement tests that we use to track student progress through the grades. What we must ask ourselves as education practitioners, policymakers, and consumers is whether we like what we see in that mirror. Indeed, we should be asking to what extent the textbook is a sufficient vehicle for delivering as much of the curriculum as it is currently called upon to deliver.

   Language Arts. The fact that there are only two articles
in this section appears to illustrate very well the problem,
mentioned above, of the textbook not being recognized as an
important factor influencing the quality of classroom instruction. One author (Graves, Item 261) focuses the lack of attention to writing in language arts texbooks and another auth-
or (Donsky, Item 260) concludes that this has been a problem
since the turn of the century, since little has changed since
then. Indeed, the recent crop of language arts textbook programs read more like writer's handbooks than stimulators and
guides to the writing of effective prose and poetry.

   Mathematics. The recent rejection by California of all
mathematics textbook programs submitted for adoption was pres-
aged by a number of the articles in this section. Several of
authors found mathematics textbooks to be insufficient as sole
sources of the mathematics curriculum because of inconsistent
topic coverage and the lack of attention to open-ended problem
solving and other higher order cognitive processes.

   Reading. The emphasis here is on the teaching of reading
comprehension, in contrast to previous period when much was
written about phonics. Two booklength sets of articles tackle
problems related to the quality of comprehension instruction
offered by basal textbook programs, along with related topics.
Another group of authors identified a problem with reading
basals similar to a major problem with language arts and mathematics programs: just as the acts of writing and open-ended
problem solving are missing in those subject areas, one can
search nearly in vain for much attention to the actual act of
reading in the midst of the sequences of skills found in most
reading texts.

   Science. Most of the authors in this section agree that
contemporary textbook programs do not reflect the true nature
of science. Considerable concern is shown with perceived superficiality in wide topic coverage, a stress on memorization,
and too little attention to introducing students to the processes of science. In contrast to the inquiry-oriented science programs developed in the 1960s, the elementary and juni-
or high science textbooks offer mainly cookbook-style recipes
in place of bona fide experiments. In addition, potentially
controversial topics such as human reproduction and evolution
are avoided, clear presentations of the relationships (and
differences) between science and technology are few and far
between, and social and environmental issues relating to sci-

ence are given cursory treatment at best.

Social Studies. Judging from the number of entries in
this section, history and social studies textbooks have received more attention than those in any other subject area.
Most of the entries are articles dealing with the adequacy of
content coverage in specific topic areas. Exceptions include
the Fitzgerald book (Item 346), which covers a half-century in
time and also deals with textbook writing and publishing, the
Reyes article on critical thinking (Item 369), and the article
by English (Item 345) on the caliber of writing in social
studies texts.

Ideology and Controversy

Ideology A good deal of concern has been expressed over
the reliance of the educational system on textbooks in the
shaping of instruction, so we should also be concerned about the
philosophical or ideological emphases that authors and publishers have given to much textbook content. This section
contains a number of articles dealing with how the selection
and presentation of content in textbooks serve as vehicles
for transmitting national (or regional, group) values and
thereby shape learner perceptions of their own society and the
societies of other nations. The articles describe how the
writers of textbooks have influenced the political socialization of learners, how changes in American foreign policy have
impact on the focus of secondary level history and geography
textbooks, and how the content of elementary school readers
transmits cultural values and attitudes. Textbooks from other
nations are also included as exemplified by articles describing analyses by scholars from the United States and the Soviet
Union of how each country is represented in the other's textbooks and one on the politicization found in the content of
civics texts in Norway.

Controversy and Censorship. As the numerous articles,
commentaries, and books abstracted in this section attest,
censorship of textbooks and library books is of major concern
to educators and other professionals. The items in this section fall into three groups. One group describes attempts at
censorship or reports the results of surveys indicating the
scope of censorship or its targets (usually library books).
The second group consists of articles explaining First Amendment principles, detailing court cases and their implications

for those dealing with censorship, and providing suggestions
about procedures for dealing with complaints about materials,
and so forth. The third group consists of articles and other
materials that discuss the issues surrounding judgments as to
what is appropriate knowledge for children of different ages,
the responsibilities of parents in determining what kinds of
moral and social concerns children should be exposed to, and
the role and responsibilities of educators and educational
policy makers in mediating between the demands of various community constituents and state and national expectations.

Very few of the materials abstracted in this volume fall
into the third group. This seems particularly unfortunate because, as with most educational issues, censorship issues in-
volve more than a strident defense of the First Amendment and
professional privilege, a position which, unfortunately, the
authors of most of the articles take. It is to be hoped that
more articles wrestling with difficult questions such as appropriate knowledge and school responsibility will be forth-
coming. In addition, it would be good to see more articles
describing the effects of challenges to controversial materials on textbook content.

Evolution and Creationism. While the actors involved in
censorship and the treatment of controversial issues come from
diverse backgrounds and in reality defy easy categorization,
this is not the case with evolution and creationism. Since
before the Scopes trial, the theory of evolution has been a
bone of contention between those Americans (and their representative organizations) who believe in the literal interpre-
tation of the Bible, on the one hand, and biologists, other
scientists, and lay people who believe that the theory (or
theories) of evolution represents a rational, evidence- based
explanation for the development of life on earth, on the
other. The first group subsumes science in religion; the
latter group attempts to keep religion and science separate.

Groups opposing evolution have had widespread impact on
science textbooks. In fact, until the publication of high
school biology textbooks based on the federally sponsored Biological Sciences Study Commission (BSCS) projects, the coverage of evolution in both elementary and secondary textbooks
was extremely limited--even to the extent that Darwin was not
mentioned and the term "evolution" could not be found in the
index. The BSCS textbooks use evolution as a major
organizing principle and there is evidence that in
reaction to this many school districts continue to

use the outdated textbooks. Despite , the expressed expectations of commentators, biologists, and educational researchers
to the contrary, the authors of other biology textbooks have
not followed the BSCS example. Moreover, the State of
California recently rejected elementary and junior high level
science textbook programs because of inadequate coverage of
evolution, among other topics. Articles in this volume document the efforts of special interest groups to exclude the
teaching of evolution, or to demand "equal time" for the
teaching of creationism.

There is evidence that a number of post-BSCS textbooks
have succumbed to anti-evolution pressure, especially in the
face of state laws (as in Texas) that force publishers to
state that evolution is only one of many theories of human
development. In elementary school science textbooks, evolution is almost completely shunned. In high school biology
some current textbooks--as many did in previous times--ex-
clude Darwin and give limited coverage to the topic.

Unfortunately, little work has been done that gives us in-
sight into just how publishers who equivocate reconcile the
ideological position of the proponents of creationism with
school knowledge based on the science disciplines.

TEXTBOOK PRODUCERS AND CONSUMERS

I. TEXTBOOKS AND SCHOOL PROGRAMS

A. TEXTBOOK USE AND CURRICULUM ROLE

001.   Bagley, W.C. (1931). The textbook and methods of
        instruction. In The textbook in American education
        (Item 201), 7-26.

        Reviews reports from the 1890s to the 1920s citing
        heavy and deleterious dependence on textbooks. Also
        gives the results of a survey on textbook dependence
        conducted for the yearbook in which 539 lessons were
        observed. A high proportion of lessons were recita-
        tions that were mainly reproductions of an assignment
        from a single textbook.

002.   Beck, I.L., & McKeown, M.G. (1987). Getting the most
        from basal reading selections. The Elementary
        School Journal, 87, 343-356.

        Examines the instructional procedures found in the
        preparation and questioning components of directed
        reading lessons. Suggests that teachers who see that
        their understanding of issues related to text compre-
        hension will be better able to tailor instructions to
        student needs.

003.   Cahen, L.S., Filby, N., McCutcheon, G., & Kyle, D.W,
        (1983). Class size and instruction. New York:
        Longman.

        In studying an elementary school, the researchers
        found heavy dependence on textbooks. The textbook
        approach and its instructional design determined
        classroom instruction.

004.   Cronbach, L.J. (1955). The text in use. In Text
        materials in modern education (Item 179), 188-216.

Discusses three levels of curriculum and instruction with the least desirable, but most prevalent (Level III), being a heavy dependence on the textbook. Most teachers are "average" and therefore tend to rely on textbooks. Publishers claim that textbooks represent the "master teacher" and that instructional problems arise when teachers do not follow them closely.

005.   Deighton, L.C. (1971). Textbooks: role in education. The encyclopedia of education (Item 181), 210-214.

Gives an overview of the functions, range and variety, value (including limitations and "essentiality") of textbooks, contemporaneous and historically.

    *   Downey, M.T. (1983). Beyond the era of the new social studies: putting the present in perspective. The Social Studies. (Cited below as Item 156).

006.   Duffey, G.D., Roehler, L.R., & Putnam, J. (1987). Putting the teacher in control: basal reading textbooks and instructional decision making. The Elementary School Journal, 87, 357-366.

Holds that instructional decision making is impeded by district level requirements that teachers conform to procedures laid down in teacher's guides. Describes ways of helping teachers make independent instructional decisions within the context of the scope and sequence of the basal reader.

007.   Educational Products Information Exchange Institute (1977). Report on a national study of the nature and the quality of instructional materials most used by teachers and learners (Report No. 76). New York: Author.

Reports on the basis of an extensive survey of teachers that between 70% and 90% of classroom instructional time is structured by commercial and teacher-created materials.

008.   Eisner, E.W. (1987). Why the textbook influences
            curriculum. Curriculum Review, 26(3), 11-13.

            Describes the textbook and its ancillary materials
            as serving multiple functions that reinforce its
            central role in determining curriculum content.
            Textbooks provide expertise, are "timesavers," and
            provide security for both teachers and students in
            outlining content scope and sequence.

   *   Elliott, D.L., Nagel, K.C., & Woodward, A. (1985). Do
            textbooks belong in elementary social studies?
            Educational Leadership. (Cited below as Item 345.)

   *   Engle, S.H. (1986). Late night thoughts about the new
            social studies. Social Education. (Cited below as
            Item 158).

   *   Freeman, D.J., Kuhs, T.M., Porter, A.C., Floden, R.E.,
            Schmidt, W.H., & Schwille, J.R. (1983). Do textbooks
            define a national curriculum in elementary school
            mathematics? The Elementary School Journal. (Cited
            below as Item 267.)

009.   Gross, R.E. (1952). American history teachers look at
            the book. Phi Delta Kappan (Item 193), 290-291.

            Gives results of a survey showing that 79% of Cali-
            fornia high school teachers reported following one
            textbook closely. 78% had used the same textbook for
            a decade.

010.   Jensen, J.M., & Roser, N. (1987). Basal readers and
            language arts programs. The Elementary School
            Journal, 87, 375-383.

            Argues that a successful language arts program
            requires a teacher who does not abdicate teaching
            responsibility to a reading textbook, but uses the
            textbook as one of many resources and relies upon
            personal knowledge of children, language, and teaching
            and learning.

011.   LaPointe, A. (1986). The state of instruction in
            reading and writing in U.S. elementary schools. Phi
            Delta Kappan, 68, 135-138.

Gives information from the National Assessment of
Educational Progress indicating that 95% of teachers
use workbooks every day. 90% are satisfied with their
instructional materials and 87% use the tests that
accompany their textbooks.

012.   Mason, J.M. (1983). An examination of reading
        instruction in third and fourth grades. The Reading
        Teacher, 36, 906-913.

Reports that observations of reading lessons reveal
that textbook-related comprehension lessons are seldom
taught and that sequenced or topically organized reading instruction is lacking.

013.   McCutcheon, G. (1982). Bait: the publishing industry
        has too much influence on the secondary English
        curriculum. English Journal, 71, 16.

Reports research showing that teachers are dependent
on teacher's guides and make few independent decisions
about instruction. Suggests that schools develop
alternative materials to supplement the basic text.

014.   McCutcheon, G. (1981). How do elementary school
        teachers plan? The nature of planning and
        influences on it. The Elementary School Journal,
        81, 4-23.

Research on teacher planning found heavy dependence
on textbooks and teacher's guides, with as much as 85%
to 90% of reading and mathematics activities based on
teacher's guide suggestions. In subjects such as
social studies, which were taught less often, teachers
did not rely on textbooks as much because of time constraints that forced decisions about what to teach.

015.   McCutcheon, G. (1981). Elementary school teachers'
        planning for social studies and other subjects.
        Theory and Research in Social Education, 9, 45-66.

Reports results of a study of how teachers plan
their teaching that shows that most teachers place
great faith in the textbooks they use.

016.   National Commission on Excellence in Education. (1983)
         A nation at risk: the imperative for educational re-
         form. Washington, D.C.: Government Printing Office.

         Cites one unpublished study on lack of challenge in
         some textbooks. Recommends upgrading and updating of
         textbooks to assure more rigorous content, higher
         adoption standards, requirements that publishers fur-
         nish data on effectiveness, funding for text develop-
         ment in "thin-market" areas, and more consumer inform-
         ation services for purchasers.

017.   Shannon, P. (1987). Commercial reading materials, a
         technological ideology, and the de-skilling of
         teachers. The Elementary School Journal, 87,
         308-329.

         Argues that reading experts have encouraged the use
         of basal readers as a way of incorporating scientific
         method and business procedures into instruction. The
         result has been a redefinition of reading and a re-
         duced role for both teacher and student.

018.   Shannon, P. (1982). A retrospective look at teachers'
         reliance on reading materials. Language Arts, 59,
         844-853.

         Reviews articles dealing with commercial reading
         materials that appeared in Language Arts over a 60
         year period. While commercial materials were often
         criticized, may authors felt teachers would become
         less dependent on textbooks if they made the effort.
         A brief discussion of textbook dependency concludes
         the article.

019.   Shannon, P. (1982). Some subjective reasons for
         teachers' reliance on commercial reading materials.
         The Reading Teacher, 35, 884-889.

         Reports on a survey of teachers and administrators
         to find out why teachers rely so heavily on textbooks.
         Administrators thought textbook content represented
         "science," while teachers did not. Teachers reported
         using textbooks closely because of administrator
         demands.

020.   Shannon, P. (1983). The use of commercial reading
         materials in American elementary schools. <u>Reading
         Research Quarterly</u>, <u>19</u>, 68-85.

         Reports research showing reading instruction has
         become standardized and "reified" in the basal reader
         and objective testing. This "objective" approach
         provides the school district and community with a
         measure of school success and reinforces the depend-
         ence on textbooks.

  *   Squire, J. (1962). Bait: the publishing industry has
         to much influence on the secondary English
         curriculum. <u>English Journal</u>. (Cited below as Item
         152.)

021.   Stake, R.E., and Easley, J.A., Jr. (1978). <u>Case
         studies in science education</u>, Volume II: design,
         overview, and findings. Champaign/Urbana: Center
         for Instructional Research and Curriculum Evalua-
         tion, University of Illinois, 13:59-13:61.

         Summarizes classroom study findings that, although
         the teacher was in charge of the classroom, the source
         of knowledge authority was the textbook and, for
         students "knowing was not so much a matter of
         experiencing . . . but of being familiar with certain
         information or knowing how to produce the answers to
         questions that would be asked."

022.   Venezky, R.L. (1987). A history of the American
         reading textbook. <u>The Elementary School Journal</u>,
         87, 247-265.

         Reviews the evolution of the reading textbook and
         shows how changes have occured in response to changing
         attitudes towards childhood and toward the role of the
         school in imparting competencies to learners. Topics
         include the development of the multi-text series, the
         creation and expansion of teacher's manuals, and the
         evolution of a reading curriculum.

  *   Weiss, I. (1978). 1977 national survey of science,
         mathematics, and social studies education. In
         National Science Foundation. <u>The status of pre-
         college science, mathematics, and social studies</u>

practices in U.S. schools. (Cited below as Item 172.)

023.   Westbury, I. (1985). Textbooks: an overview. International encyclopedia of education research and studies (Item 190), 5233-5234.

Characterizes the textbook as "an elusive component of schooling, at least from the point of view of conventional research and theory, describes it as an educational "tool," and argues that social constraints within the field of education have constrained educational researchers from sustained consideration of the basic issues associated with textbook use and development.

024.   Westbury, I. (1985). Textbook distribution. International encyclopedia of education research and studies (Item 190), 5230-5231.

Decribes the textbook as ubiquitous in Western educational systems and refers to studies linking student achievement to the availability of textbooks. Gives statistics on textbook distribution in less industrialized societies and finds a need for more data about the mechanisms of effective textbook distribution in those countries.

025.   Westbury, I. (1985). Textbooks, history of. International encyclopedia of education research and studies (Item 190), 5234-5235.

Gives an overview of two periods of textbook history, one associated with the emergence of the printed textbook and vernacular instruction in the 16th and 17th century and the other with the establishment of the textbook as a basic instrument for the large-scale organization of curriculum and teaching.

026.   Woodward, A. (1986). Taking teaching out of teaching and reading out of learning to read: a historical study of teacher's guides, 1920-1980. Book Research Quarterly, 2, 53-73.

Describes a study of basal reading series teacher's guides that showed the role of the teacher changed

from "professional" to "manager" over a period of
years. Guides published in the 1970s present detailed
scripts and lesson plans for teachers to follow. The
development of reading as a "managed," objective-based
collection of skills is discussed.

027.   Woodward, A. (1986). Overprogramming materials: taking
         the teacher out of teaching. American Educator, 10,
         26-31.

         Discusses the changing status of the teacher from
         professional to implementer of pre-set lessons as
         detailed in teacher's guides.

B. TEXTBOOK SELECTION

028.   Beattie, C. (1966). Judging the worth of curriculum
        materials: a preview approach. Journal of
        Curriculum Studies, 18, 299-309.

        Discusses criteria (such as achievable and worth-
        while objectives and accurate and comprehensive sub-
        ject matter) by which to judge the educational value
        of curricular materials and outlines results of apply-
        ing this criteria to three separate programs.

029.   Bowler, M. (1978). Textbook publishers try to please
        all, but first they woo the heart of Texas. The
        Reading Teacher, 31, 514-518.

        Represents a portion of a 1976 six-part series of
        articles on textbook merchandising and selection in
        the United States. This part discusses how textbook
        publishers attempt to tailor their programs to meet
        the needs of the market and how the content of basal
        reading books is influenced by demands of states whose
        districts select from an approved statewide list.

030.   Clary, L.M., & Smith, S.J. (1986). Selecting basal
        reading series: the need for a validated process.
        The Reading Teacher, 39, 390-394.

        Discusses the lack of uniformity in the textbook
        selection process among states and recommends that
        points of view of diverse groups such as reading
        specialists, teachers, parents, students and local
        boards of education be considered along with state
        department of education requirements.

031.   Cody, C.B. (1986). A policymaker's guide to textbook
        selection. Alexandria, VA: National Association of
        State Boards of Education.

Assists policymakers in thinking about new standards
for books and book selection by reviewing pertinent
issues such as the relationship between the selection
process and the quality of books, currency and
accuracy of content, etc. Also contains speech
summaries and recommendations of the 1985 NASBE and
CCSSO Conference.

032.   Coffey, W.L. (1931). Legislative agencies for textbook
        selection. In The textbook in American Education
        (Item 201), 249-273.

Discusses textbook selection procedures for this
period of time including classifying states according
to the particular agencies given authority by each
state to adopt textbooks; providing a comprehensive
list of adoption provisions used by the various
states, and separate summaries of the legislative
provisions in effect in states where a) state control
prevails, b) state and district control prevails, c)
county control prevails, and d) district control
prevails.

033.   Coffey, W.L. (1931). Judicial opinion on textbook
        selection. In The textbook in American education
        (Item 201), 275-289.

A historical document (1931), this chapter discusses
the leading textbook cases during this period of time
which illustrate the motives and legal principles
evolved through the settlement of issues growing out
of the administration of textbook laws.

034.   Coffey, W.L. (1949). Selection and purchase of
        textbooks. In Textbooks in education. New York:
        The American Textbook Publishers Institute, 75-92.

Summarizes how textbooks were selected in early
times and describes how the selection process has
become increasingly structured up to this period
(1949). Also included are fictitious letters written
to a textbook selection committee by a textbook sales
representative and by a publishing company executive.

035.   Courtland, M.C. (1983). A case study of the Indiana
        State reading textbook adoption process.
        Bloomington: Indiana University.

        Describes a study in which three major areas were
        pursued: a) documentation of the adoption process,
        b) the perceptions of state Commissioners and textbook
        reviewers regarding the adoption process, and c) a
        description of the reviewing process.

036.   Cowles, H.M. (1976). Textual materials evaluation: a
        comprehensive checklist. Foreign Language Annals,
        9(4), 300-303.

        Presents and discusses a two-page Textual Materials
        Evaluation Checklist used to identify the degree and
        manner in which programs provide a number of consider-
        ations germane to evaluating textual materials such as
        sequence of presentation, clarity of statements, feed-
        back, etc.

037.   Crane, B. (1975). The "California effect" on
        textbook adoptions. Educational Leadership, 32,
        283-285.

        Relates how textbook revisions required by
        California educators become incorporated in the
        publishers' national editions.

038.   DeRose, J.V., & Whittle, J.R. (1976). Selecting
        textbooks: a plan that worked. The Science Teacher,
        43(6), 38-40.

        Discusses a science textbook selection procedure
        that involved a steering committee of subject-area
        specialists outside the school district with a
        district-wide teachers' committee. Each committee had
        separate duties and responsibilities which resulted in
        a collaborative decision-making process.

039.   Dole, J.A., Rogers, T. & Osborn, J. (1987). Improving
        the selection of basal reading programs: a report of
        the Textbook Adoption Guidelines Project. The
        Elementary School Journal, 87, 283-298.

        Summarizes the results and piloting of A Guide to

Selecting Basal Reading Programs by four textbook
adoption committees and addresses the role of the
project in the larger endeavor to improve reading
instruction in the elementary schools.

040.   Durkin, D. (1987). Influences on basal reader
          programs. The Elementary School Journal, 87,
          331-341.

Describes how past critics of the schools have been
an effective force for change in reading instruction
and emphasizes that current instruction in basal reading programs will improve only when school districts
and textbook selection committees make effective pedagogy their highest priority.

041.   Eash, M., Talmage, H., & Walberg, H. (1975).
          Evaluation of instructional materials. Report No.
          45. Princeton: ERIC Clearinghouse on Texts,
          Measurement, and Evaluation.

Examines the evaluation of instructional materials
from three points of view: a) an analytic system
focused on the quality and completeness of the instructional design of the materials and their fit with
the school curriculum; b) a reference file of instructional design constructs of materials on the market;
and c) the significance of materials evaluation in
meeting the goals of two different curriculum
designs.

  *   Edmonson, J.B. (1931). The ethics of marketing and
          selecting textbooks. In Whipple, G.M. (Ed.). The
          textbook in American education. (Cited below as
          Item 110.)

042.   Educational Products Information Exchange Institute,
          EPIE Materials Reports, Volumes IX-XIV, 1975-1980.

Provide instructional design descriptions of textbook programs in secondary social studies (1975), bi-
lingual education (1976), elementary and junior high
science (1976), elementary reading (1977), elementary
social studies (1978), secondary U.S. history (1978-
79), and elementary and secondary language arts
(1980). (Textbook PRO/FILEs provide similar informa-

tion on elementary and junior high programs in language arts, mathematics, reading, science, and social
studies published during the early 1980s.)

043.   English, R. (1980). Politics of textbook adoption.
        Phi Delta Kappan, 62, 275-278.

        Surveys some of the competing forces that influence
        the quality of textbooks such as state adoption
        procedures that "homogenize and sterilize" textbooks,
        demands from "super states" such as California and
        Texas, mandates of special interest groups, and
        profit-margins of textbook publishers.

044.   Exline, J.D. (1984). Science textbook adoption
        process. The Science Teacher, 51(1), 92-93.

        Discusses results of a survey taken of members of
        the Council of State Science Supervisors about
        textbook programs and adoption procedures. Findings
        identified a desire by supervisors for field-tested
        and inquiry-based programs that are currently not
        being met by textbook publishers.

045.   Farr, R., & Tulley, M.A. (1985). Do adoption
        committees perpetuate mediocre textbooks? Phi Delta
        Kappan, 66, 467-461.

        Discusses the varied approaches taken by local
        districts nationwide in textbook selection and offers
        five recommendations to improve existing adoption
        practices.

046.   Farr, R., Tulley, M.A., & Powell, K. (1987). The eval-
        uation and selection of basal readers. The Elemen-
        tary School Journal, 87, 267-281.

        Begins with a review of how basal readers determine
        the reading curriculum, and then discusses weaknesses
        in the textbook selection process such as lack of
        teacher training and disproportionate influences of
        special interest groups, and concludes by setting
        forth several recommendations for improving the
        process including training for selectors.

047.   Finley, F. (1979). Selecting a new science program?
         Science and Children, 17(2), 16-17.

         Defines administrator and teacher roles in textbook
         selection and summarizes the selection process used by
         one school district.

048.   Fitzgibbons, S.G. (1985). The role of professional
         associations in textbook selection: The National
         Council for the Social Studies. Book Research
         Quarterly, 1(2), 73-81.

         Argues the need for professional groups such as the
         National Council of Social Studies and teacher
         education institutions to share their expertise in
         processes with state and local educators.

049.   Follett, R. (1985). The school textbook adoption
         process. Book Research Quarterly, 1(2), 19-23.

         Views the competitive textbook adoption process as
         one that generates sales for textbook producers who
         are able to meet the needs of selection committees.
         Also states that if schools were willing to spend more
         for instructional materials, publishers would have the
         financial resources for better research, development,
         and testing of materials.

050.   Guenther, J. & Hansen, P. (1977). The status of
         elementary social studies series adoptions in four
         midwestern states. Journal of Social Studies
         Research, 1(2), 43-52.

         Discusses results of a survey taken of midwestern
         school districts' social studies series adoption
         procedures in which 69% of the districts surveyed
         adopted a single textbook series. Suggests that
         adoption rate and general satisfaction are two
         variables often overlooked in the adoption process.

 *   Hausman, H.J. (1976). Choosing a science program for
         the elementary school. (Cited below as 164.)

051.   Jevitz, L., & Meints, D.W. (1979). Be a better book
        buyer: guidelines for textbook evaluation. Journal
        of Reading, 22, 734-738.

        Presents a 12-part checklist in which users indicate
        Yes, No, or Not Applicable to statements about read-
        ablility, concepts, presentation of material, visual
        aids, cultural and sexual bias, teaching manuals, and
        other topics.

052.   Keith, S. (1985). Choosing textbooks: a study of
        instructional materials selection processes for
        public education. Book Research Quarterly, 1(29),
        24-37.

        Describes and analyzes selection procedures from a
        national perspective, reviews recent trends in the
        California selection process, and considers upcoming
        issues such as the potential for a national consensus
        of instructional materials and the dominance of text-
        books in instruction.

053.   Keith, S. (1981). Politics of textbook selection
        (Project Report No. 81-A7). Washington, D.C.:
        National Institute of Education.

        Examines the process of textbook selection in terms
        of prior research and in light of the political and
        social debate it generates. The paper is organized
        around four main themes: a) the relationship between
        textbooks and the profit making enterprises of text-
        book publishers, b) state level control over the con-
        tent and selection of textbooks, c) groups with power
        to influence which textbooks will be selected, and d)
        the relationship between the educational bureaucracy
        and the general public.

054.   Kirst, M.W. (1984). Choosing textbooks: reflections of
        a state board president. American Educator, 8(2),
        18-23.

        Underscores the need for careful selection by
        reviewing the changing emphases given to selection by
        state adoption committees which continue to focus on
        appearance and pedagogy rather than on content.

055.   Krause, K.C. (1976). Do's and don'ts in evaluating
          textbooks. Journal of Reading, 20, 212-214.

          Recommends using the SMOG Formula to determine
          readability levels and lists eighteen items that
          should be considered in evaluating textbooks.
          Considerations listed include the clarity with which
          captions are written, presence of chapter summaries,
          highlighting of new vocabulary, etc.

056.   Lang, L.Z. (1985). The adoption process of reading
          texts in Virginia and its application in the
          Arlington public schools. Book Research
          Quarterly, 1(2), 49-72.

          Describes and compares the separate adoption
          processes used by the state of Virginia and by the
          Arlington school division. Major differences were
          that Arlington decided which series to evaluate and
          provided for a piloting of the materials. Includes
          models of the evaluation instruments.

057.   Leonard, W.H., & Lowery, L.F. (1976). A criterion for
          biology textbook selection. The American Biology
          Teacher, 38, 477-479.

          Describes the use of an instrument to categorize
          questions in four biology textbooks according to
          frequency, relevance to the direct experience of the
          student, cognitive level, and kind of scientific
          process required of student to complete the question.

058.   Lewis, R.M. (1984). Choosing textbooks: inspect before
          you select. The American School Board Journal,
          171(9), 42-43.

          Presents ten recommendations to serve as basic
          guidelines for the textbook selection process.

059.   McLeod, R.J. (1979). Selecting a textbook for good
          science teaching. Science and Children, 17(2),
          14-15.

          Recommends and provides guidelines for choosing a
          science text which is experiment-dependent, teaches
          science processes, and contains content that is

appropriate and meaningful to the age of the learner.

060.   Milburn, G. (1971). How are social studies
         curriculum materials evaluated? History and Social
         Science Teacher, 12, 237-241.

         Discusses the characteristics and strengths and
         weaknesses of two modes of analytic schema, the
         Curriculum Materials Analysis System and the Vallence
         schema, which can be used to evaluate social studies
         materials.

061.   Miller, J.W. (1986). Evaluation and selection of basal
         reading programs. The Reading Teacher, 40, 12-17.

         Reports that teachers participating in a textbook
         selection study tended to use their observations in a
         predictable decision making process.

062.   Moyer, W.A., & Mayer, W.V. (1983). As Texas goes, so
         goes the nation: a report on textbook selection in
         Texas. Washington, D.C.: People for the American
         Way.

         Includes a description of the Texas adoption process
         and its national significance, reviews background on
         the Gablers and their influence along with other pro-
         testers in 1982, describes the 1982 adoption proce-
         dure, and makes eight recommendations to improve the
         selection process.

063.   Moyer, W.A., & Mayer, W.V. (1985). A consumer's Guide
         to Biology Textbooks. Washington, D.C.: People for
         the American Way.

         Includes an overview of the Texas textbook selection
         process, evaluations and criticisms of 18 general,
         academic, and advanced biology textbooks submitted in
         April 1984 for adoption in Texas, testimony to the
         Texas Board of Education by two scientists, and
         refutions of creationism theory.

064.   Moyer, W.A. (1985). How Texas rewrote your textbooks.
         The Science Teacher, 52(1), 23-27.

         Relates how pressure groups in Texas, such as the

Gablers and People For the American Way, have influenced the coverage by publishers of such topics as evolution and human sexual reproduction in elementary and secondary science textbooks and how this influence affects the content appearing in textbooks purchased by school districts nationwide.

065.   Muther, C. (1985). Alternatives to piloting textbooks. Educational Leadership, 42, 79-83.

Recommends that districts ask publisher agents about their own and competitors' programs, consult with users of programs, and examine revisions based on field testing.

066.   Muther, C. (1984). How to evaluate a basal textbook: the skills trace. Educational Leadership, 42, 79-80.

Recommends doing a skills trace of one skill throughout all textbooks in a series (or in several series) as a means to become familiar with the introduction, practice, and testing of the skill and to distinguish treatment of the skill between different programs.

067.   Muther, C. (1985). The service guarantee means help from the publisher. Educational Leadership, 42, 79-81.

Recommends and describes a legally binding agreement between textbook publisher and purchaser to reduce ordering errors, ensure appropriate use, and provide personalized services.

068.   Muther, C. (1984). The skills trace. Educational Leadership, 42, 82-85.

Offers critical questions that will help textbook selectors determine the visual appeal, durability, copyright changes, teaching suggestions, ease of use, and authorship of programs.

069.   Muther, C. (1986). Textbook deals: is your board putting cost before curriculum? The American School Board Journal, 173(1), 32-34.

Discusses various textbook deals between publishing companies and school districts that emphasize cost-cutting measures over selection of materials appropriate to learners and suggests ways to circumvent this problem.

070.   Muther, C. (1985). What every textbook evaluator should know. Educational Leadership, 42, 4-8.

Stresses that school districts should first define the role textbooks are to play in the curriculum and to select textbooks on that basis. An overview of the development and marketing of programs by publishers is presented.

  *   National Commission on Excellence in Education. (1983). A nation at risk. (Cited above as Item 016.)

071.   Ney, J. (1982). Evaluating the linguistic components of secondary language arts textbooks. English Journal, 71(3), 36-37.

Presents the broad list of questions developed in 1977 by the committee established by the NCTE Commission on the English Language to provide teachers and curriculum planners with appropriate guidelines to stimulate discussion and critical examination of the content of language arts textbooks.

072.   Osborn, J., & Stein, M. (1981). Textbook adoptions: a process for change. In Harris, T.L., & Cooper, E.J. (Eds.). Reading, thinking, and concept development. New York: College Entrance Examination Board, 257-271.

Reviews weaknesses of textbook-dominated curricula, proposes steps to improve textbook adoption procedures, and summarizes current efforts in this direction.

073.   Osborn, J. & Stein, M. (1985). Basal reading programs: development, effectiveness, and selection. Book Research Quarterly, 1(2), 38-48.

Discusses the development, differences in content

and approach, demands of pressure groups, and general
weaknesses affecting reading programs, and describes a
set of single-topic pamphlets being developed to aid
textbook adoption committees.

074.   Phipps, N.J. (1984). Autonomy or uniformity? Phi
          Delta Kappan, 65, 416-418.

          Describes how the diversity and autonomy in select-
          ing instructional materials by three small school dis-
          tricts was lost when they were merged into one large
          district which became increasingly uniform in its
          approach to materials selection.

075.   Powell, D.A. (1985). Selection of reading textbooks at
          the district level: is this a rational process?
          Book Research Quarterly, 1(3), 23-35.

          Reports preliminary results of the selection proce-
          dures used by two Indiana school districts during the
          1983 reading textbook adoption.

076.   Robbins, R.H. (1980). Choosing the right basal reader.
          Curriculum Review, 19(5), 395-399.

          Discusses how cost and censorship pressures affect
          the production and selection of reading basals and
          provides a list of criteria by which to evaluate pro-
          grams.

077.   Rosencranz, A.D. (1985). Who decides what pupils read?
          Compact, 9(6), 5-7.

          Reviews the tiered system of textbook review taking
          place in state adoptions and discusses the trend
          toward increased local autonomy in many districts.

078.   Ryan, L. (1977). Judging textbooks: the Asia Society
          Project. The Social Studies, 68, 236-240.

          Summarizes the intent of the Asia Society Textbook
          Evaluation Project to locate social studies textbooks
          which offered an unbiased coverage of Asian and other
          cultures and recommends that selectors consider the

following in choosing textbooks: Did people with
Asian studies background write the book? When was the
book written? What is the attitude of the textbook
toward other cultures in the book?

079.   Sabol, J.W. (1977). Selecting instructional materials.
        English Journal, 66(1), 9-14.

        Offers a humorous, yet serious, five-part guideline
        for selecting instructional materials.

080.   Schomburg, C.E. (1986). Texas and the social studies
        texts. Social Education (Item 374), 58-60.

        Describes how the needs of Texas educators and
        special interest groups affect textbook content
        nationwide and overviews the Texas adoption system.

081.   Smith, P. (1971). Textbooks: selection and
        distribution. The encyclopedia of education (Item
        181), 220-224.

        Gives paragraph-length descriptions on topics encom-
        passing selection, adoption, publisher's representa-
        tives, distribution, manufacturing standards, state
        printing, contracts, and college textbooks.

082.   Tully, M.S. (1985). A descriptive study of the intents
        of state-level textbook adoption processes.
        Educational Evaluation and Policy Analysis, 7(3),
        289-308.

        Examines the intent, efficacy, and impact of state
        level textbook adoption policies and processes.

083.   Tully, M.A. & Farr, R. (1985). The purpose of state
        level textbook adoption: what does the legislation
        reveal? Journal of Research and Development in
        Education, 18 (2), 1-6.

        Discusses results of a content analysis of the text-
        book adoption statutes of the 22 state adoption states
        to gain insight into the intent or purpose of state
        level textbook adoption practices. Results of the
        study suggest that the intent "may be to control the
        marketing practices of the publishing industry."

084.   Tully, M.A. & Farr, R. (1985). Textbook adoption:
         insight, impact, and potential. Book Research
         Quarterly, 1(2), 4-11.

         Discusses the historical development of, and the
         advantages and disadvantages associated with, existing
         textbook adoption processes and suggests areas in
         which improvement is needed before the adoption pro-
         cess can be considered a means of achieving education-
         al reform.

085.   Tyson-Bernstein, H., & Woodward, A. (1986). The great
         textbook machine and prospects for reform. Social
         Education (Item 374), 41-45.

         Discusses the problems and pressures associated with
         state adoption procedures which are aggravated by a
         lack of cooperation and communication between textbook
         publishers, state and local agencies, public school
         districts, and researchers of educational issues.

086.   Weiner, L. (1979). Warning: textbooks are not made--
         or used--in heaven. English Journal, 68(9), 7-10.

         Begins by cautioning selectors to be wary of pub-
         lisher claims of textbook authorship and goes on to
         recommend that selection committees obtain guidelines
         from district administration, consult outside sources
         providing textbook critiques, and to devise an evalua-
         tion form.

087.   Westbury, I. (1985). Textbook approval. Internation-
         al encyclopedia of education research and studies
         (Item 190), 5223-5225.

         Gives brief accounts of surveys of national
         policies, textbook adoption in the United States, and
         textbook adoption in historical perspective.

088.   Westbury, I. (1985). Textbook selection: pedagogical
         considerations. International encyclopedia of
         education research and studies (Item 190),
         5231-5233.

         Summarizes recent research bearing on problems in

textbook writing and selection, including pressure
group influence, readability, and pedagogical structure, and with particular emphasis on the matter of
"considerate" text.

089.   Winograd, P. & Osborn, J. (1985). How adoptions of
        reading textbooks works in Kentucky: some problems
        and some solutions. Book Research Quarterly, 1(3),
        3-22.

Describes the textbook adoption process used in
Kentucky in which a Textbook Selection Criteria
Committee for Reading works cooperatively with the
State Textbook Commission and includes an eight-part
five-point rating scale with which to evaluate basal
reading series.

II. THE PRODUCTION AND MARKETING OF TEXTBOOKS

A. THE TEXTBOOK INDUSTRY

090.   American Textbook Publishers Institute (1949).
        Textbooks in education. New York: Author.

        A description of the editorial and manufacturing
        steps in producing a textbook.

091.   Apple, M.W. (1984). The political economy of text
        publishing. Educational Theory, 34, 307-319.

        Textbooks transmit cultural knowledge. The nature
        of the publishing industry, its profit seeking and
        textbook management result in standardized and
        "managed" texts.

092.   Archibald, G. (1900). Joel Dorman Steele. New York:
        A.S. Barnes & Company.

        A biography of one of the major high school textbook
        writers of the late 19th century. Gives a number of
        anecdotes related to the writing of Steele's history
        series.

093.   Bierstedt, R. (1955). The writers of textbooks. In
        Text materials in modern education (Item 179),
        96-126.

        Discusses the role of textbook authors in
        transmitting knowledge and culture. Notes that
        authors are subject to ideological and professional
        pressures and these influence textbook content.

094.   Black, H. (1967). The American schoolbook. New York:
        William Morrow.

        Covers problems involved in creating and selling
        textbooks, constraints on the publication of innova-
        tive materials, and how publishers deal with contro-

versial issues, among other topics. Contemporary
examples are used such as a case study of the creation
of Harper's highly successful Today's Basic Science.

095.   Boller, P.F., Jr. (1980). High school history: memoirs
of a Texas textbook writer. Teachers College
Record, 82, 317-327.

As author of a U.S. history textbook published in
the 1960s, Boller refutes many of the claims made by
Fitzgerald (347), and says his textbook contained few
of the problems cited by Fitzgerald. Tells of the
unsuccessful efforts by special interest groups to
block the book's adoption in Texas.

096.   Bowler, M. (1976). For texts, this is "open
territory." The Baltimore Sun (October 4), A1-A3.

Describes textbook selling and purchasing in the so-
called "open territory" of Maryland. With no state-
wide adoptions, publisher representatives must reach
24 public school districts and hundreds of buildings.

097.   Bowler, M. (1976). School books are peddled like
autos. The Baltimore Sun (October 3), A1, A20.

The salesman's job is to deprecate the competition
and, at the same time, imply that his company's older
books are not as good as the new ones. Sales techniques such as wining and dining are discussed.

098.   Bowler, M. (1978). The making of a textbook.
Learning, 6(3), 38-43.

Describes the process whereby textbooks are written,
edited, produced, and marketed. The various compro-
mises publishers make in producing textbooks to accom-
modate market demands are detailed.

099.   Bragdon, H.W. (1969). Dilemmas of a textbook writer.
Social Education, 33, 292-298.

The author of a popular U.S. history series relates
his experiences in negotiating with publishers and
writing the text. Notes that some constraints were
imposed on him; for example, the Civil War had to be

called the War Between the States as a concession to
the Southern market. Indicates that subsequent editions sported new covers and a variety of "improve-
ments."

100.   Bragdon, H.W. (1978). Ninth edition adventures with a
        textbook. Independent School, 37(3), 37-41.

        Retrospective report on the writing of a U.S.
        history textbook. Attributes the success of the text
        to its emphasis on politics and minimal treatment of
        the colonial period. Notes that new edition saw
        increasing use of color and graphics and that "gim-
        micks" such as folded maps and overlays were transient
        features that appeared in one edition and disappeared
        in the next.

101.   Brammer, M. (1967). Textbook publishing. In Grannis,
        C.B. (Ed.). What happens in book publishing. New
        York: Columbia University Press, pp. 320-349.

        Describes publishers and editors as the major
        players in creating and writing textbooks. Also
        discusses the role of authors, the importance of
        textbook design, and the purchasing of textbooks.

102   Broudy, E. (1975). The trouble with textbooks.
        Teachers College Record, 77, 13-14.

        A former textbook editor's view of the pressures
        influencing textbook production. Uses examples from
        the industry to show the roles of authors, editors,
        and sales staff. Discusses the influence of the
        market and adoption states.

103.   Brown, E. (1952). The role of the textbook salesman.
        Phi Delta Kappan (Item 193), pp. 276-277.

        A senior social studies editor for Harcourt Brace
        describes the crucial role of the textbook salesman in
        a competitive market. Most importantly, salesmen
        bridge the gap between the advanced thinking in educa-
        tion embodied in new texts and actual practice.

  *   Cohen, B. (1986). Censoring the sources. School
        Library Journal. (Cited below as Item 403.)

104.   Cubberly, E.P. (1931). The state publication of
          textbooks. In The textbook in American education
          (Item 201), 235-248.

          Reviews the success of the printing of textbooks by
          states such as California and Kansas and notes the few
          economic and educational benefits of such a practice.

105.   Dahlin, R. (1981). A tough time for textbooks.
          Publishers Weekly (August 7), 28-32.

          Explores publisher reactions to special interest
          group pressures. Although publishers were reluctant
          to talk, they did note that the pressures are not new
          and span both liberal and conservative groups.
          Discusses the impact of the Gablers' efforts to
          promote creationism.

106.   Davis, B. (1985). Scholastic work: many forces shape
          making and marketing of a new schoolbook. The Wall
          Street Journal (January 3), 1.

          Reports on the launching of the hoped-for block-
          buster textbook, America: the glorious republic, by
          Columbia historian Henry F. Graff. On the basis of
          market research indicating that the market leader
          (Harcourt's Rise of the American nation) was weak,
          Houghton Mifflin spent $800,000 to produce a competing
          text.

107.   Davis, J.E., & Hawke, S.D. (1986). Boards and
          publishers should collaborate on the design of
          curriculum materials. The American School Board
          Journal, 173(1), 35-36, 40.

          Advocates "needs-based" publishing on the assumption
          that schools rarely get materials that really fit
          their needs.

  *   Downey, M.T. (1980). Speaking of textbooks. The
          History Teacher (Cited below as Item 343).

108.   Duffey, T.M., & Waller, R. (Eds.). (1985). Designing
          usable texts. New York: Academic Press.

          Contains Items 140, 141, 155, and 196

109.   Edgerton, R.B. (1969). Odyssey of a book: how a social
        studies text comes into being. Social Education,
        33, 279-286.

        Covers authors, contractors, author-editor relation-
        ships, major stages in preparation of a text, supple-
        mentary items, and myths concerning textbooks.

110.   Edmonson, J.B. (1931). The ethics of marketing and
        selecting textbooks. In The textbook in American
        education (Item 201), 199-220.

        Reports on a survey of educators and publishers on
        marketing and selection practices. Ethical standards
        relating to the marketing of textbooks was considered
        to be higher than in previous years.

111.   Educational Products Information Exchange Institute
        (1980). Deciphering LVR. Stonybrook, NY: Author.

        Chronicles the demands for the integration of learn-
        er feedback in the textbook development process, the
        creation of a taskforce of educators and publishers to
        study the problem, and the publication of pilot
        Learner Verification and Revision guidelines. Notes
        that, while several states enacted laws mandating pub-
        lisher use of LVR, these laws soon became dead
        letters.

112.   Educational Products Information Exchange Institute
        (1970). Textbooks: reviews and a look at the
        industry (Report No. 29). New York: Author.

        An overview of developments in the publishing indus-
        try. Notes that, while innovative materials are some-
        times developed, most companies keep to the tradition-
        al textbook, which can guarantee a good return on
        investment.

   *   Fitzgerald, F. (1979). America revised: history
        schoolbooks in the twentieth century. (Cited below
        as Item 346).

   *   Follett, R. (1985). The school textbook adoption
        process. Book Research Quarterly. (Cited above as
        Item 049.)

113.   Fox, W. (1985). Textbook publishing is profitable but
         controlled. The Boston Globe (December 1), 8-9.

         Reports that publishing is becoming increasingly
         profitable and will continue to be so into the next
         decade. Discusses the cost of producing textbooks and
         the importance of adoption states. Notes that text-
         book publishing is a no-risk business--innovative
         materials are rarely successful and thus companies
         take no risks. Describes how one company faced bank-
         ruptcy because it departed from the standard.

114.   Frymier, J. (1983). A tribute to publishers.
         Education Forum, 47, 388-391.

         While agreeing that textbook quality is poor, espe-
         cially in the treatment of controversial issues, the
         author argues that the public and selection commit-
         tees, not publishers, are responsible for this situa-
         tion.

115.   Goldstein, P. (1978). Changing the American school-
         book: law, politics, and technology. Lexington, MA:
         Lexington Books.

         Covers many aspects of the textbook industry
         (product development, marketing, economics), the pur-
         chase and use of textbooks, and the place of textbooks
         in the electronic classroom.

116.   Graham, A. (1986). Elementary school social studies
         texts: an author-editor's viewpoint. Social
         Education (Item 374), 53-55.

         While noting that social studies textbooks are
         excellent, identifies some disturbing trends affecting
         textbook quality: buyers generally have unreasonable
         expectations about the textbooks they are selecting,
         including recent copyright dates and challenging books
         with low readability levels.

117.   Gray, A. (1952). Lift the workbook cover. Phi Delta
         Kappan (Item 193), 286-287.

         Argues for greater use of workbooks. Holds that
         workbooks provide meaningful practice, adequate drill

for each child, skill application, self-instruction,
and individual attention. Notes that an American
Textbook Publishers Institute report recommends workbooks for every child for reading, spelling, language,
penmanship, and arithmetic.

118.   Hawke, S.D., & Davis, J.E. (1986). A small publisher's
        perspective on the textbook controversy. Social
        Education (Item 373), 68-69.

        Asserts that the role of the small company is to
        fill those needs that large companies ignore. Argues
        that small publishers can be very responsive to school
        needs and can take pedagogical risks.

119.   Henderson, H. (1987). Reading by ear. Chicago's Free
        Weekly Reader (January 2), 1-6.

        Describes the Open Court Publishing Company and
        discusses the company's founding and its innovative
        and controversial mathematics and reading programs.

120.   Henderson, K. (1985). A maverick publishing house that
        bucks the big business trend. The Christian Science
        Monitor (October 25), B8.

        Reports that, because a small publisher caters to
        the independent school market, it is able to produce
        textbooks of higher quality than the standard texts.
        With low overhead, a company can publish texts with
        sales of only 2500 per year. Company owners welcome
        the movement to increase public high school standards
        and note that some public schools are now purchasing
        textbooks from them.

121.   Henry, N.B. (1931). The cost of textbooks. In
        The textbook in American education (Item 201),
        221-234.

        Reports the costs of textbooks per student over a
        15-year period.

122.   Henry, N.B. (1931). The problem of publishers in
        making and marketing textbooks. In The textbook in
        American education (Item 201), 175-198.

Publishers report a number of problems and issues in textbook publishing: authors are not always accurate, some educators allow their names to be used on text-books they have not authored, and educator insistence on recent copyright dates (5 years) present problems in the production of high quality books and state adoption practices.

123.   Jantzen, S.L. (1979). What textbooks will be like in 1985. Media and Methods, 15(5), 70-72.

Publishers undertake extensive surveys of teachers and interview key educators to gauge the textbook market. The author predicts that inquiry-based texts, individualized learning materials, and other innova-tive textbooks will not be published. Dominant texts will be those combining factual content with skills and low readability levels.

124.   Jensen, F.A. (1931). The policies of publishers in marketing textbooks. In The textbook in American education (Item 201), 163-173.

Discusses the important role of the sales represen-tative in marketing textbooks.

125.   Jensen, F.A. (1931). The selection of manuscripts by publishers. In The textbook in American education (Item 201), 79-92.

Gives results of a survey of publishers that found authors are selected through personal contact with field representatives. Unsolicited manuscripts are rarely accepted and the amount of editorial revision varies from company to company.

126.   Jovanovich, W. (1969). The American textbook: an unscientific phenomenon--quality without control. The American Scholar, 38, 227-239.

Presents a brief history of publishing in the United States and an overview of recent developments.

 *   Keith, S. (1981). Politics of textbook selection. (Cited above as Item 053.)

127.   King, L.W. (1952). Economics of textbook publishing.
        Phi Delta Kappan (Item 193), 254-256.

        Reports the results of a survey of publishers
        responsible for 90% of textbook sales. Findings indi-
        cate that schools spend one per cent of their budgets
        on textbooks. A breakdown of the cost of textbook
        production for a "typical" publisher is given.

128.   Knowlton, P.A. (1950). What is wrong with textbooks?
        Phi Delta Kappan, 33, 56-58.

        While praising the general quality of textbooks, a
        publishing executive identifies some problem areas:
        overuse of color for marketing rather than instruc-
        tional purposes, re-copyrighting textbooks too soon,
        timid content because of special interest group pres-
        sure, the trend to give away too many materials, and
        the overdesigning of teacher's guides.

129.   Komoski, P.K., & Woodward, A (1985). The continuing
        need for learner verification and revision of
        textual material. In Jonassen, D.H. (Ed.). The
        technology of text, Volume 2. Englewood Cliffs, NJ:
        Educational Technology Publications, 396-417.

        Gives an overview of learner verification and revi-
        sion (LVR) as applied to the production of textbooks
        and microcomputer courseware. Various examples are
        given showing the beneficial effects of using LVR to
        make textbooks more understandable to learners.

130.   Kuya, D. (1977). The unacceptable face of publishing.
        The Times Educational Supplement (June 22), 16.

        Argues that many new textbooks produced in the
        United Kingdom are more colorful versions of earlier
        ones; however they continue to portray racist stereo-
        types. Notes that a number of large and independent
        publishers are now producing more sensitive materials.

131.   Lacy, D. (1980). Revising America: a symposium at the
        National Endowment for the Humanities. The History
        Teacher, 13, 570-574.

        In responding to Fitzgerald's (347) criticism of the

poor academic quality of U.S. history textbooks, a
senior executive from McGraw-Hill attributes the
situation to the marketplace and competition.

132.   Lawler, T.B. (1938). Seventy years of textbook
        publishing: a history of Ginn & Company. Boston:
        Ginn & Company.

        Presents a history of the textbook company, includ-
        ing a chapter on history textbook author Philip Van
        Ness Myers, whose books dominated the market for 40
        years.

133.   Livengood, W.W., & Loveland, G. (1952). To whom it may
        concern. Phi Delta Kappan (Item 193), 278-282.

        Two editors provide information for budding textbook
        authors. Describes how publishers differ in policies:
        some do in-house editing; others have minimal editor-
        ial staff. Explains why only books with wide market
        appeal are published.

134.   Marquand, R. (1985). Textbook maker's view: the ground
        rules have to be changed. The Christian Science
        Monitor (October 25), B7.

        The owner of a development company that develops and
        revises textbooks for major publishers claims that
        textbooks are as good as educators allow them to be.
        Because of market demands, textbooks must be revised
        on a two-year cycle, a difficult task that results in
        the cutting of corners, since it realistically takes
        five years to create a high quality textbook.

135.   Marriott, R.J. (1977). School books: who decides, and
        how? Reading, 11(3), 23-34.

        Gives an overview of textbook publishing and produc-
        tion in the United Kingdom.

136.   McCaffrey, A.J. (1971). Textbooks: production. The
        encyclopedia of education (Item 184), 214-220.

        Discusses functions of textbooks, their range and
        variety, value, limitations, and "essentiality."

137.   McConnell, J.V. (1978). Confessions of a textbook
         writer. American Psychologist, 33, 159-169.

         Describes his particular approach to writing an
         introductory psychology textbook. Notes that when
         writing a textbook, demands from five audiences--
         students, instructors, peers, publisher, and self--
         must be taken into account.

  *   McCutcheon, G. (1982). Bait: the publishing industry
         has too much influence on the secondary English
         curriculum. English Journal. (Cited above as Item
         013.)

138.   Muther, C. (1986). Textbook deals: is your board
         putting cost before curriculum? The American School
         Board Journal, 173(1), 32-34.

         Discusses the buying and selling of textbooks, with
         emphasis on how publishers give away much free mate-
         rial in order to convince buyers they are getting a
         good deal when, in fact, these costs are passed on to
         the consumer. Describes other marketing techniques.

  *   National Commission on Excellence in Education (1983).
         A nation at risk. (Cited above as Item 016.)

139.   Nietz, J.A. (1952). Why and how do textbooks get
         bigger? Phi Delta Kappan (Item 193), 251-253.

         Textbooks generally increased in size during the
         19th century and the first two decades of this
         century. Thereafter, rapid increases took place. For
         example, recent secondary level U.S. history textbooks
         average 639 to 824 pages compared to 295 pages for
         books published between 1795 and 1885. Similar
         findings were made for science books.

140.   Olson, D.R. (1985). On the designing and understanding
         of written texts. Designing usable texts (Item
         108), 3-15.

         The text mediates between reader and speaker and, as
         such, creates the illusion of autonomy, authority, and
         objectivity. Rather than being based upon theory,
         textbooks are accumulations of practical experience

and evolving technology designed for a general market.
Inevitably, textbooks cannot address the individual
child in a personal, direct way.

141.   Orna, E. (1985). The author: help or stumbling block
          on the road to designing usable texts? In Designing
        usable texts (Item 108), 19-41.

        Assuming that the author is "in control" of the text
        he or she writes, describes what research and experi-
        ence indicate can be done to make a text more under-
        standable to the reader.

142.   Patch, C. (1985). Changing times in picture research.
        Publisher's Weekly (July 5), 30-32.

        Because of cost concerns, many publishers are clos-
        ing their picture research departments and contracting
        with independent consultants.

143.   Pearson, R.M. (1952). Can textbooks be subversive?
        Phi Delta Kappan (Item 193), 248-250.

        A Macmillan vice president finds that, while text-
        books may be subject to pressures from special inter-
        est groups, they reflect current trends, theories, and
        political realities. Suggests that educators look at
        modern textbooks when making judgments since those
        published during World War II reflected a very differ-
        ent (and at the time acceptable) perspective regarding
        the U.S.S.R.

144.   Redding, M.F. (1963). Revolution in the textbook
          industry. Los Angeles: Department of Audiovisual
        Instruction, National Education Association.

        Discusses the history of textbook publishing and
        notes that the industry is at a crucial point in its
        development. Educators need to let publishers know
        what they require--be it paperback texts, full-color
        layout, or whatever.

145.   Reid, J.M. (1969). An adventure in textbooks,
          1924-1960. New York: R.R. Bowker Co.

        Autobiography of a long-time executive of a major

textbook company. Relates anecdotes concerning textbook adoption in Texas in the 1930s, the recruitment
of writers, and other topics.

146.   Richey, H.G. (1931). The professional status of
        textbook authors. In The textbook in American
        education (Item 201), 67-77.

        While recognizing that there are many influences on
        textbooks, asserts that authors play an important role
        in determining the character of the text. Research
        indicates that between 1876 and 1926 an increasing
        percentage of authors have been from universities and
        colleges.

147.   Rist, M. (1986). But collaboration could be costly,
        complicated. The American School Board Journal,
        173(1), 36, 40.

        Scott, Foresman and Houghton Mifflin executives
        respond to the Davis and Hawkes (107) proposal for
        need-based publishing. Argues that such materials
        would be very expensive and, besides, there is no need
        for such a system since a wide variety of materials
        are already available.

148.   Rout, L. (1979). But out with the hippies! The Wall
        Street Journal (September 5), 1, 28.

        Discusses the new textbook America! America! which
        cost Scott, Foresman $500,000 to develop. Market
        research indicated that the public was looking for a
        textbook that reflected a more pluralistic society,
        hence the text included black cowboys, women pirates,
        and Haight-Ashbury hippies, as well as the inclusions
        and exclusions of content demanded by such states as
        Florida and Texas.

  *   Schneider, D.O., & Van Sickle, R.L. (1979). The status
        of the social studies: a publisher's perspective.
        Social Education. (Cited below as Item 372.)

149.   Schorling, R., & Edmonson, J.B. (1931). The techniques
        of textbook authors. In The textbook in American
        education (Item 201), 27-66.

Reports on a survey of textbook authors who use "scientific techniques." Instructional principles derived from research in learning and the specific disciplines are enumerated.

150.   Schramm, W. (1955). The publishing process. In
         Text material in modern education (Item 179),
         129-165.

Gives an overview of the textbook industry that includes sections on economics, production, competition from alternative media, and the roles of editors, authors, and sales representatives.

151.   Schuster, E.H. (1985). Textbooks: there never has been
         a golden age. Education Week (March 6), 40.

Using examples from his own textbooks, the author disputes the claim that textbooks have declined in quality. Notes that authors must constantly make decisions regarding what should be in textbooks.

  *   Simmons, J.S. (1981). Proactive censorship. English
         Journal. (Cited below as Item 436.)

152.   Squire, J. (1962). Bait: the publishing industry has
         too much influence on the secondary English
         curriculum. English Journal, 71, 17.

Asserts that publishers may have less influence than is thought in determining classroom instruction. Textbooks range from excellent to poor and it is the educator's responsibility to select the best. Text-books and teacher's guides usually reflect up-to-date research on learning and instruction, however, teacher often choose not to follow textbook suggestions. (See also Item 013.)

153.   Talmage, H. (1986). Creating instructional materials:
         the textbook publisher as connecting link.
         Curriculum Review, 26(1), 8-10.

Discusses the important role of the interpreter (textbook writer) in relating the work of scholars to the needs of students. Publishers act as the connect-

ing link between scholars, interpreters, and teachers.
The publishers are especially important in finding out
what a broad cross-section of teachers want in a textbook.

*   Venezky, R.L. (1987). A history of the American
        reading textbook. The Elementary School Journal.
        (Cited above as Item 022.)

154.   Westbury, I. (1985). Textbook development. Interna-
        tional encyclopedia of education research and
        studies (Item 190), 5227-5230.

        Discusses commercial textbook publishing,
        government-sponsored textbook development, and
        instructional systems development.

155.   Wright, P. (1985). Editing: policies and processes.
        In Designing usable texts (Item 108), 63-96.

        Asserts that the editor is often the crucial person
        in ensuring that the text communicates knowledge to
        the intended audience, but notes that technical devel-
        opments facilitating the transmission of author text
        directly to printing may limit the input of editors.

*   Zuidema, H.P (1981). Less evolution, more creationism
        in textbooks. Educational Leadership. (Cited below
        as Item 472.)

B. INNOVATION AND REFORM

*   Agostino, V.R., & Barone, W.P. (1985). A decade of
     change: elementary social studies texts. Social
     Studies. (Cited below as Item 333.)

156.   Downey, M.T. (1983). Beyond the era of the new social
     studies: putting the present in perspective. The
     Social Studies, 74, 6-10.

     Describes some of the effects of the "new social
     studies" movement on secondary level history programs,
     including the presence of inquiry exercises and social
     science concepts in textbooks. Suggests that "dealing
     with the reality of the textbook-centered classroom is
     one of the major challenges facing history educators
     in the 1980s."

157.   Dyrli, O.E. (1981). Should we scrap lab-centered
     science programs? Learning, 9(7), 34-35, 39.

     Gives reasons for the movement away from laboratory-
     centered elementary science programs: return to "the
     basics," the cost of updating, interest in technology
     and "traditional" science content, and lack of profes-
     sional support. Proposes the systematic laboratory
     program components as supplements to textbook pro-
     grams.

158.   Engle, S.H. (1986). Late night thoughts about the new
     social studies. Social Education (Item 373),
     20-22.

     Argues that the main reason the "new social studies"
     programs are not being used is that teachers "are
     poorly prepared by their own education to confront the
     controversy and uncertainty that is the real bone and
     sinew of scholarship" and democratic ideology "is not
     as universally accepted by our people as our language
     would lead us to believe."

159.   Feldrake, H.J. (1966). Student acceptance of the new
         mathematics programs. The Arithmetic Teacher, 13,
         14-20.

         Presents the results of a study to determine the
         feelings of upper- and average-ability students to-
         wards the new mathematics programs. Found that the
         upper group had a greater preference for the new pro-
         grams than the average group, that many chose the
         "new" because they found it more interesting, and that
         others chose the "old" because they found it easier to
         understand.

160.   Fetsko, W. (1979). Textbooks and the new social
         studies. The Social Studies, 70, 51-55.

         Presents the results of a study comparing U.S. and
         world history textbooks published in 1955-1961 with
         those published in 1970-1977 to determine the influ-
         ence of the "new social studies." More than 50% of 14
         characteristics of new social studies were found in
         the later texts, whereas less than 10% were found in
         texts published in the earlier period. A greater
         degree of change was noted in the U.S. history texts
         than the world history texts.

161.   Haas, J.D. (1977). The era of the new social studies.
         Boulder: ERIC Clearinghouse for Social Studies/
         Social Science Education and the Social Science
         Education Consortium.

         Provides a history of the New Social Studies,
         including the curriculum materials projects, the ways
         in which their products were introduced to the
         profession, and appraisals made of the NSS projects.

162.   Hahn, C.L. (1976). Familiarity with and perceived
         characteristics of 'New Social Studies' materials.
         Three studies on perception and utilization of 'new
         social studies' materials (Item 163), 9-27.

         Reports results of a questionnaire study of 911
         secondary social studies materials selectors to
         determine the extent of their familiarity with any of
         22 new social studies programs, their perceptions of
         the materials, and the relationship between these

perceptions and their willingness to adopt the
materials.

163.   Hahn, C.L., Marker, G.W., Switzer, T.J., & Turner, M.
        J. (1977). Three studies on perception and
        utilization of 'new social studies' materials.
        Boulder: Social Science Education Consortium.

        Contains items 162, 170, and 171.

164.   Hausman, H.J. (1976). Choosing a program for the
        elementary school. Washington, D.C.: Council for
        Basic Education.

        Describes federal support for the development of
        alternatives to textbook programs in the 1960s,
        including ESS, SAPA, SCIS, MINNEMAST, COPES, and
        USMES.

  *   Helgeson, S.L., Blosser, P.E., & Howe, R.W. (1977).
        The status of pre-college science, mathematics, and
        social science education: 1955-1975, Volume I:
        science education. (Cited below as Item 318).

165.   Jackson, P.W. (1983). The reform of science education:
        a cautionary tale. Daedalus, 112(2), 143-166.

        Discusses the curriculum reform movement of the
        1960s and 1970s in the context of broader federal
        intervention in educational affairs and reviews the
        literature on the accomplishments of the movement and
        the reasons for its failures. Includes analyses of
        the influence of the science projects on the textbook
        market.

  *   Janis, J. (1972). Textbook revisions in the sixties.
        Teachers College Record. (Cited below as Item
        357.)

166.   Kissock, C., & Falk, D.R. (1978). A reconsideration of
        'Attributes and adoption of new social studies
        materials.' Theory and Research in Social Education,
        6(3), 56-70.

Reports results of a study to analyze the
relationship between the degree of the potential
adopter's perceived influence and attitudes toward,
and adoption of, new social studies materials.

167.   Marker, G.W. (1980). Why schools abandon 'new social
         studies' materials. Theory and Research in Social
         Education, 7(4), 35-56.

Reports results of a survey of seven school staffs
to determine why use of three textbooks with a "heavy
inquiry orientation" was discontinued. Found that
unrealistic user expectations concerning student
interest and involvement, the departure of a major
adoption advocate, and manner of use differing from
that intended by the developers were the main factors.

168.   Schneider, D.O., & Van Sickle, R.L. (1979). The status
         of the social studies: the publishers' perspective.
         Social Education, 43, 461-465.

Reports results of a questionnaire survey of 36
major publishers of social studies materials. Re-
spondents viewed the field as relatively stable, with
a return to traditional topics, although some changes
in content emphases were evident.

169.   Shaver, J.P., Davis, O.L., & Anderson, R.C. (1979).
         The status of social studies education: impressions
         from three NSF studies. Social Education, 43,
         150-153.

Summarizes some findings of three NSF studies
(Weiss, 172; Suydam & Osborne, 272; Stake & Easley,
021). Those findings having to do with textbooks
include: a) materials from federally funded projects
of the 1960s and 1970s were not being selected for
classroom use (only 25% of teachers were using a mini-
mum of one program), b) the dominant instructional
material continues to be the conventional textbook, c)
the curriculum is mostly history and government, with
geography at K-8, d) the dominant modes of instruction
continue to be large group, teacher-controlled recita-
tion and lecture based primarily on the textbook, and
e) the "knowing" expected of students is largely in-
formation-oriented: to be successful, students have to

reproduce not only the content but the language of the textbook.

170.   Switzer, T.J., Lowther, M.A., Hanna, W.M., & Kidder,
        R.D., Dissemination and implementation of social
        studies project materials. Three studies on
        perception and utilization of 'new social studies'
        materials (Item 163), 29-52.

        Gives results of a questionnaire study of 252
        secondary social studies teachers in five states to
        determine what variables are significantly related
        to their learning about, examining, and using these
        materials.

171.   Turner, M.J., and Haley, F., Utilization of 'new
        social studies' curriculum programs. Three studies
        on perception and utilization of 'new social
        studies' materials (Item 163), 53-101.

        Reports results of a study to determine the extent
        of utilization of nine sets of "new social studies"
        materials in four states, the characteristics of the
        teachers using these materials, and teachers' percep-
        tions of success in using the nine programs.

 *   Vanek, E.P., & Montean, J.J. (1977). The effect of two
        science programs (ESS and Laidlaw) on student
        classification skills, science achievement, and
        attitudes. Journal of Research on Science Teaching.
        (Cited below as Item 331.)

172.   Weiss, I.R. (1978). Report of the 1977 national survey
        of science, mathematics, and social studies educa-
        tion. Washington, D.C.: U.S. Government Printing
        Office, 68-99.

        Reports findings of survey on: a) federally-funded
        curriculum materials, including sources of informa-
        tion, state dissemination of information, and use of
        the materials in schools; and b) the use of text-
        books/programs, including the most-used ones, copy-
        right dates, and those involved in selection.

173.   Welch, W.W. (1979). Twenty years of science curriculum
         development: a look back. In Berliner, D.C. (Ed.).
         Review of Educational Research 7. Washington, D.C.:
         American Educational Research Association, 282-306.

         Reviews and discusses studies of science curriculum
         development, including the characteristics of the cur-
         riculum products and the development strategy that
         went into producing them, factors influencing their
         adoption and use, and evidence of their impact on
         schools and students. Conclusions related to the
         assertion that the science classroom of today is
         little different from the one 20 years ago.

174.   Wiley, K.B., & Race, J. (1977). The 'new social
         studies. The status of pre-college science,
         mathematics, and social science education, Volume
         III. Boulder, CO: Social Science Education
         Consortium, 194-197, 206-208, 291-323.

         Summarizes articles and papers covering the charac-
         teristics, criticisms, and impact of the "new social
         studies."

EVALUATION AND CRITICISM OF TEXTBOOKS

III.   **GENERAL DISCUSSION AND SPECIAL TOPICS**

A. GENERAL REFERENCES

175.   Bernstein, H. (1984). Bad writing and "mentioning" are
        seen as major flaws of textbooks. Basic Education,
        26(3), 1-5.

        Summarizes several key issues that contribute to
        poor quality textbooks. Includes discussions, with
        examples, of the pervasive problems of text written
        following readability formulas and superficial
        coverage ("mentioning") of numerous topics.

176.   Burton, W.H., Gray, W.S., Hanna, P.R., Manwiller, Van
        Toor, J., & Ford, C.A. (1952). Needed research on
        textbooks. Phi Delta Kappan (Item 193), 297-300.

        Burton sees "undue dependence on texts" and suggests
        research on the use of a wide range of resources.
        Gray calls for further research on those aspects of
        textbooks that influence their ease or difficulty.
        Hanna wants to find ways of strengthening the textbook
        as a instrument by which the reader is helped to
        observe his own experiences and to organize his own
        system of ideas. Manwiller offers 23 questions for
        textbook selectors to ask. Van Toor asks eight
        questions about textbook production, selection, and
        use. Ford asks for research in the use of color and
        varying formats as well as studies of various ways of
        using textbooks in the classroom.

177.   Chall, J.S. (1977). An analysis of textbooks in
        relation to declining SAT scores. New York: The
        College Board.

        Presents results of a historical and correlational
        study of the instructional quality and difficulty of
        textbooks and SAT scores. Argues that a relationship
        exists between periods when "easy" textbooks were

published and later declining SAT scores.

*   Ciolli, R. (1983). The textbook wars. Newsday
        Magazine. (Cited below as Item 401.)

178.   Cole, J.Y., & Stricht, T.G. (Eds.) (1981). The
        textbook in American society. Washington, D.C.: The
        Library of Congress.

        Contains summaries of conference presentations on
        textbooks, including points of view of publishers,
        researchers, and educators about the design and
        quality of textbooks, the publishing industry, and
        prospects for change.

179.   Cronbach, L.J. (1955). Text materials in modern
        education. Urbana: University of Illinois Press

        Contains Items 004, 093, and 150.

180.   Davis, O.L., Jr. (1962). Textbooks and other printed
        materials. Review of Educational Research, 32,
        127-141.

        Reviews research reports about textbooks and printed
        materials that appeared between 1957 and 1961.
        Includes analysis of content in the basic subjects,
        textual variables (e.g., readability and typography),
        the use of print materials (inluding workbooks and
        trade books).

181.   Deighton, L.C. (Ed.) (1971). The encyclopedia of
        education, Volume 9. New York: The Free Press,
        pp. 211-224.

        Contains Items 005, 081, and 136.

182.   DeSilva, B. (1986). Schoolbooks: a question of quality
        [4-part series]. The Hartford Courant (June 15-18).

        Describes the problems with elementary and secondary
        level textbooks on the basis of reports and interviews
        with educators, administrators, and publishers.

183.   Doyle, D.P. (1984). The "unsacred" texts. The
        American Educator, 8(2), 8-13.

        Denounces the mediocrity and amorality of today's
        textbooks. Attributes this situation to the breakdown
        of a consensus about what children should learn that
        has resulted in a textbook market characterized by
        competing demands and values and an industry that
        accommodates these demands by producing textbooks that
        will offend no one.

184.   Dronka, P. (1985). Will a third round of reform take
        the textbook to task? ASCD Update, 27(6), 1, 6-7.

        Presents an overview of the problems of mentioning,
        copyright, selection, and readability.

  *   Elliott, D.L., Nagel, K.C., & Woodward, A. (1985). Do
        textbooks belong in elementary social studies?
        Educational Leadership. (Cited below as Item 344.)

185.   Elson, R.M. (1964). Guardians of tradition: American
        schoolbooks of the 19th century. Lincoln:
        University of Nebraska Press.

        Reports on a study of over 1000 of the most popular
        textbooks used in grades one through eight. Main
        headings encompass God and Nature, The Nature of Man,
        Schoolbooks and "Culture, and Social Experience (eco-
        nomic and political concepts, social values, and
        social reform movements).

  *   Fitzgerald, F. (1979). America revised: history
        schoolbooks in the twentieth century. Boston:
        Little, Brown. (Cited below as Item 346.)

186.   Graves, M.F., & Slater, W.H. (1986). Could textbooks
        be better written and would it make a difference?
        American Educator, 10(1), 36-42.

        Starting with the premise that textbook prose is
        dull and boring, the authors asked three groups--text
        linguists, college composition instructors, and
        editors of Time-Life--to rewrite a passage on the
        Vietnam War taken from a grade 11 history textbook.
        High school students recalled 40% more of the passage

rewritten by the Time-Life editors compared to minor
gains for the other rewritten passages.

187.   Gwynn, J.M. (1960). The influence of the textbook.
         Curriculum principles and social trends. New York:
         Macmillan Co., 206-237.

         Discusses various aspects of textbook quality, role,
         and influence on education. Gives special attention
         to attempts at censoring textbooks. An extensive
         contemporary bibliography is provided.

188.   Hilton, E. (1969). Textbooks. In Ebel, R.L. (Ed.).
         Encyclopedia of Educational Research. New York:
         Macmillan Co., 1470-1478.

         Offers overview sections on textbooks: history,
         evolution, functions and use, readability, publish-
         ing, and textbooks in other countries.

189.   Hockett, J.A. (1979). Materials of instruction. Review
         of Educational Research, 29, 177-184.

         Reviews research reported in period 1956-1958. For
         printed materials, includes topics of readability,
         social studies and language arts, and arithmetic and
         science. Calls for further research, given the
         importance of instructional materials and the amount
         of money spent on them. (See also Item 192.)

190.   Husen, T., & Postlethwaite, T.N. (1985). The
         International Encyclopedia of Education Research and
         Studies. New York: Pergamon Press.

         Contains items 023, 024, 025, 087, 088, 154, 199,
         200, 258.

191.   Marquand, R. (1985, October 25). Textbooks: debate
         heats up over the growing push for reform. The
         Christian Science Monitor (October 25), B1, B5-6.

         A report on the debate over the quality of textbooks
         and efforts at reform.

192.   Otto, H.J., & Flournoy, F. (1956). Printed materials.
         Review of Educational Research, 26, 115-124.

Reviews studies analyzing textbook content, including interest factors, textbooks and international understanding, presentation and format, and physical characteristics of printed materials. Briefly discusses textbook uses and adoption policies and practices.

193.   Phi Delta Kappan (1952). Textbooks (Issue Theme). *Phi Delta Kappan*, *33*, 290-301.

Contains items 009, 103, 117, 127, 133, 139, 143, 176, 353, and 364.

194.   Reynolds, J.C. (1976). American textbooks: the first 200 years. *Educational Leadership*, *3*, 274-276.

Gives a brief overview of the historical role of the textbook in transmitting values, describes the evolution of a modern biology textbook, and discusses the impact of conflicting values and attitudes on the contemporary textbook scene.

195.   Reynolds, J.C. (1981). Textbooks: guardians of nationalism. *Education*, *102*(1), 37-42.

Explores the relationship between textbooks and nationalism, especially social studies textbooks. Suggests that an awareness of this relationship "can assist in developing more effective textbooks in the future, by incorporating the best thinking" of various pressure groups and textbook critics.

196.   Sticht, T. (1985). Understanding readers and their use of texts. In *Designing usable texts* (Item 108), 315-340.

Notes that texts have a very different function depending on whether the reader is in school or at work. The skills the individual needs to interpret and use text information are very different in these two types of situations.

*   Tyson-Bernstein, H., & Woodward, A. (1986). The great textbook machine and prospects for reform. *Social Education*. (Cited above as Item 085.)

197.   Vitz, P. (1985). Textbook bias isn't of a
            fundamentalist nature. The Wall Street Journal
            (December 26), 6.

            Describes a study of elementary reading and elemen-
            tary and secondary social studies texts in which cer-
            tain ideological biases were found. The traditional
            nuclear family was often excluded, no conservative
            male political figures or post-World War II business-
            men were found. Religion was not included in U.S.
            history accounts after the American Revolution.
            Argues for more choice in schools to alleviate this
            situation.

198.   Warming, E. (1982). Textbooks. In Mitzel, H.E. (Ed.).
            (1982). Encyclopedia of Educational Research, Volume
            4. New York: The Free Press, 1932-1936.

            Provides summaries of selected research on text and
            prose learning, selection and adoption, controversy
            and censorship, and the textbook industry, and future
            prospects.

199.   Westbury, I. (1985). Textbook content. The Interna-
            tional Encyclopedia of Education Research and
            Studies (Item 190), 5226-5227.

            Discusses textbooks as sources of information about
            various subject fields and as a medium for arranging
            that subject matter for the purpose of teaching.
            Textbooks often serve to define school subjects in
            ways which may be at odds with the scholarship in the
            related fields and make it difficult to introduce new
            developments in knowledge into the schools.

200.   Westbury, I. (1985). Textbooks: an overview. Inter-
            national encyclopedia of education research and
            studies (Item 190), 5233-5234.

            Characterizes the textbook as "an elusive component
            of schooling," at least from the point of view of con-
            ventional research and theory, describes it as an
            educational "tool," and argues that social constraints
            within the field of education have kept educational
            researchers from sustained consideration of the basic
            issues associated with textbook use and development.

201.   Whipple, G.M. (1931). <u>The textbook in American</u>
        <u>education</u>, 30th yearbook of the National Society
        for the Study of Education, Part II. Bloomington,
        IL: Public School Publishing Co.

        Contains Items 001, 032, 033, 104, 110, 121, 122,
        124, 125, 146, and 149.

B. READABILITY

202. Ames, W.S., & Bradley, J.M. (1981). An in-depth study of the readability of a social studies textbook. The Social Studies, 72, 77-81.

Reports the results of a readability study of one junior high school U.S. history textbook that revealed a) a wide range of readability variation, b) a lack of progression throughout the book, and c) considerable intra-chapter variation.

203. Armbruster, B.B., The problem of "inconsiderate text." Comprehension instruction (Item 287), 202-217.

Presents results of research on characteristics of text that affect learning from text and learning important information from text. Illustrates with excerpts from actual content area textbooks and draws implications for practitioners of text factors related to learning.

204. Armbruster, B.B., & Anderson, T.H. (1983). Analysis of science textbooks: implications for authors. In Robinson, J.T. (Ed.). Research in science education: new questions, new directions. Louisville: CERE/ERIC, 21-53.

Argues that certain characteristics of text can optimize learning, given that the learner has sufficient background knowledge and engages in the appropriate studying activities. Identifies the characteristics of the text that empirical research has shown to affect learning outcomes. Makes recommendations for writing and evaluating the prose in a textbook.

205. Armbruster, B.B., Osborn, J.H., & Davison, A.L. (1985). Readability formulas may be dangerous to your textbooks. Educational Leadership, 42, 18-20.

Outlines major shortcomings of reliance on readability formulas as indices of text difficulty. These
formulas fail to take into account characteristics
such as content difficulty and organization of ideas,
which affect comprehension, or to acknowledge that
readability levels vary widely within a single
textbook.

206.   Baumann, J.F. (1986). Effect of rewritten content
         textbooks passages on middle grade students'
         comprehension of main ideas: making the
         inconsiderate considerate. Journal of Reading
         Behavior, 18, 1-21.

         Describes a study in which one passage from each of
         four fifth-grade science textbook series was presented
         to students in two versions: a) an original (inconsid-
         erate) version and b) a rewritten (considerate) ver-
         sion. Found some evidence that rewritten passages
         enhanced student ability to reconstruct or generate
         main ideas; however, there was no effect on a main
         idea recognition task.

207.   Bradley, J.M., Ames, S.A., & Mitchell, J.M. (1980).
         Intrabook readability: variations within history
         textbooks. Social Education, 44, 524-528.

         Reports on an examination of the readability levels
         of common topics in eight junior high school U.S.
         history textbooks and the implications this has for
         educators.

208.   Chambers, F. (1983). Readability formulas and the
         structure of text. Educational Review, 35(1), 3-13.

         Suggests that factors such as conceptual difficulty
         and interest level be incorporated into readability
         formulas in addition to factors such as the word and
         sentence level. Recognizing the difficulty of
         quantifying such information, the author recommends at
         least mapping out these information structures.

209.   Crismore, A. (1984). The rhetoric of textbooks:
         metadiscourse. Journal of Curriculum Studies, 16,
         279-296.

Defines metadiscourse as a rhetorical style and discusses its application to the writing of social studies texts. Gives examples by summarizing a comparative study of the use of informational and attitudinal
metadiscourse in nine textbooks dealing with social
studies topics.

210.   Dale, E., & Chall, J.S. (1948). A formula for predict-
        ing readability. Educational Research Bulletin, 27,
        11-20.

Reviews some of the earlier readability formalas
(e.g., Lorge, Flesch) and describes the process
involved in developing the Dale-Chall readability
formula.

211.   Davison, A., (1884). Readability--appraising text
        difficulty. Learning to read in American schools
        (Item 275), 239-292.

Focuses on the use of readability formulas to assess
reading difficulty in instructional materials as well
as to identify sources of difficulty that may be
altered in ways that make text easier to understand.

212.   Davison, A., & Kantor, R.N. (1982). On the failure of
        readability formulas to define readable texts: a
        case study from adaptations. Reading Research
        Quarterly, 2, 187-209.

Presents findings of a comparison of original and
adapted versions of four texts showing that changes
such as splitting complex sentences into component
clauses and changing vocabulary items to conform to
readability formula levels make adapted texts harder
to understand. Advises against the implicit use of
readability formulas as guides to writing texts and
recommends experimental research to define the real
factors underlying readability.

213.   Dawkins, J. (1956). A reconsideration of the Dale-
        Chall formula. Elementary English, 33, 515-519.

Criticizes the Dale-Chall readability formula for
providing misleading guidance to textbook publishers
by focusing on sentence length rather than on factors

such as paragraph structure and complex subject
matter, that also influence reading difficulty. The
article is followed by a reply from Edgar Dale and
Jeanne Chall.

214.   Elliott, P.G., & Wiles, C.A. (1980). The print is part
          of the problem. School Science and Mathematics, 80,
          37-42.

          Argues that the readability formulas used by pub-
          lishers of secondary mathematics textbooks tend to un-
          derestimate the difficulty of reading in mathematics.
          Supports this argument with the results of the admin-
          istration of a Cloze test to 91 certified mathematics
          teachers indicating that textbooks appear to imbed
          mathematic concepts "in reading that is even difficult
          for trained teachers of mathematics to process inde-
          pendently."

215.   Feldman, M.J. (1985). Evaluating pre-primer basal
          readers using story grammar. Educational Research
          Journal, 22(4), 527-547.

          Discusses findings from story grammar research in
          which text found in pre-primer basals was compared to
          text that conformed to the rules of the Johnson and
          Mandler story grammar in order to determine whether
          text that follows a well-formed story structure is
          more easily read than a basal reader text that
          deviates from an ideal story structure.

216.   Froese, V. (1981). Judging global readability. The
          Alberta Journal of Educational Research, 27(2),
          133-137.

          Addresses the problem of judging global readability
          by matching passages of unknown difficulty to
          criterion sets of passages of known readability
          levels. Two techniques, the SEER and the Rauding
          procedures, were used by 42 teachers with varying
          years of teaching experience to rate a set of
          passages. Findings indicate that the two techniques
          resulted in different ratings, that the amount of
          teaching experience did not affect the ratings, and
          that the SEER ratings agreed with readability formula
          estimates of the same passages.

217.   Fry, E.B. (1977). Fry's readability graph: clarifica-
         tions, validity, and extension to level 17. Journal
         of Reading, 21, 242-252.

         Discusses a variety of topics, including the
         inclusion of proper nouns in word counts, the use of
         speech sounds to determine number of syllables,
         problems of validity and reliability of readability
         scores, and the extension of the Fry Readability Graph
         into the college levels.

218.   Fry, E.B. (1987). The varied use of readability
         measurement today. Journal of Reading, 30,
         338-343.

         Discusses the wide use of readability formulas to
         guide the writing of documents in fields as diverse as
         banking, advertising, insurance, and educational
         research.

219.   Harrison, C. (1986). Readability in the United
         Kingdom. Journal of Reading, 29, 521-529.

         Overviews recent work on readability and identifies
         main trends in both theory and practice that have
         emerged in the last five years. The discussion covers
         two main topic areas: a) the estimation of difficulty
         of material read by the general public and the assess-
         ment of the readability of school prose, and b) new
         research on how to measure text difficulty, microcomputer
         programs which estimate difficulty, and the results of
         studies in which students rewrite textboook prose.

228.   Horodezky, B., & Weinstein, P.S. (1981). A comparative
         analysis of vocabulary load of three provincially
         adopted primary arithmetic series. The Alberta
         Journal of Educational Research, 27(2), 123-132.

         Presents the results of a computer-assisted program
         used to investigate the degree of variability, over-
         lapping, and vocabulary load in three current primary
         arithmetic textbook programs.

221.   Irwin, J.W., & Davis, C.A. (1980). Assessing read-
        ability: the checklist approach. Journal of
        Reading, 24), 124-130.

        Describes a 36-item checklist that can be used as an
        alternative procedure for determining the readability
        levels of reading materials. Items on the checklist
        are based on currently accepted research in prose
        comprehension and have been divided into categories of
        understandability and learnability, with learnability
        subdivided into the areas of organization, motivation,
        and reinforcement.

222.   Kantor, R.N., Anderson, T.H., & Armbruster, B.B.
        (1983). How inconsiderate are children's textbooks?
        Journal of Curriculum Studies, 15, 61-72.

        Proposes some criteria for use in determining rela-
        tive 'considerateness' of children's textbooks:
        structure, coherence, unity, and audience appropriate-
        ness. Simulates the reading experience of a sixth-
        grader to illustrate how comprehension can break down.
        Urges teachers to use considerateness as an aid in
        textbook selection.

223.   Keenan, D. (1982). An evaluation of the effectiveness
        of selected readability formulas applied to
        secondary texts. Reading Horizons, 22, 123-128.
        Winter.

        Discusses the findings of a study in which students
        matched to materials of the same readability level as
        their measured reading ability performed unsuccess-
        fully on a test designed to measure their under-
        standing of grade-appropriate materials.

224.   Kennedy, K. (1979). The reading levels of high school
        physics texts. The Physics Teacher, 17, 165-167.

        Discusses the difficulty teachers have in determing
        whether a particular physics text is appropriate to
        the needs of their students and contends that the Fry
        Readability Graph has made this task simpler.

225.   Klare, G. (1985). Matching reading materials to
        readers: the role of readability estimates in
        conjunction with other information about comprehen-
        sibility. In Harris, T.L., & Cooper, E.J. (Eds.).
        Reading, thinking, and concept development:
        strategies for the classroom. New York: College
        Entrance Examination Board, 233-256.

        Overviews the development of readability formulas,
        their use, and criticism of them. Makes a number of
        practical suggestions for using readability estimates
        in conjunction with other information to determine the
        optimum match of reading textbook to learner.

226.   Klare, G. (1974-1975). Assessing readability. Reading
        Research Quarterly, 10, 62-102.

        Reviews a number of formulas and predictive devices
        in use since 1960 and concludes with suggestions for
        choosing a formula based on the following
        considerations: a) special vs. general needs, b)
        manual vs. machine application, c) simple vs. complex
        formulas, d) word length vs. word list formulas, and
        e) sentence length vs. sentence complexity. Also
        stresses the point that formulas provide good indices
        of difficulty but do not indicate causes of difficulty
        or tell how to write readable text.

227.   Lorge, I. (1951). Readability formulas--an evaluation.
        Elementary English, 28, 262-268.

        Discusses the early research of Vogel and Washburne
        that led to the development of their 1928 Grade Place-
        ment Formula, reviews readability studies by Ojemann,
        Tyler, Dale and Chall, and others. Concludes by
        stating that readability formulas are no panacea, but
        useful adjuncts in the objective evaluation of written
        and spoken materials.

228.   McKinney, E.W. (1983). Readability levels of the 1975
        third grade Macmillan basal readers. Reading
        Improvement, 20, 37-40.

        Discusses results of an analysis of third grade
        readers from Series r using a modified Flesch formula.
        Found that readability levels ranged from 3.3 to 7.8

with a mean of 4.1. Concludes that publishers need to produce more carefully designed materials and provide more reliable information on readability levels.

*   Orna, E. (1985). The author: help or stumbling block on the road to designing usable texts? In Designing usable texts. (Cited above as Item 141.)

229.   Reyes, D.J., & Smith, R.B. (1983). The role of concept learning in social studies textbook comprehension: a brief analysis. The Social Studies, 74, 85-88.

Discusses the role of concepts in the comprehensibility of written material. Suggests that making judgments regarding the potential comprehensibility of social studies textbooks requires an analysis of their method of using and presenting concepts, in particular: their assumptions regarding previous learning, how concepts are developed and presented, and the degree of concept load. Cites research to show that some textbooks fall short in all three of these areas.

230.   Ring, J.W. (1983). Technique for assessing conceptual development in chemistry texts. Journal of Chemical Education, 60(10), 893-895.

Describes a reading assessment technique in which sequential statements are analyzed for sentence structure and conceptual ordering as a basis for determining the effectiveness of the text in a classroom setting.

231.   Rowls, M.D., & Hess, R.K. (1984). A comparative study of the readability of grade seven through twelve language arts textbooks. The Clearinghouse, 57, 201-204.

Presents the results of a readability study of eight major language arts series. Results indicate that more than half of the textbooks analyzed exceeded publisher readability estimates by one or more grade levels. Five recommendations for improving the readability guidelines used in the selection of textbooks are provided.

232.   Rush, T. (1985). Assessing readability formulas and
        alternatives. The Reading Teacher, 39, 274-283.

        Discusses the characteristics of the Dale-Chall, Fry
        Graph, and Spache readability formulas as well as
        alternative text-based and read/text-based methods and
        suggests their appropriate applications.

233.   Shymansky, J.A., & Yore, L.D. (1979). Assessing and
        using readability of elementary science texts.
        School Science and Mathematics, 79, 670-676.

        Discusses the readability limitations of science
        reading materials and makes suggestions such as
        altering the sequence of teaching textbook topics and
        using multiple series between grade levels to compen-
        sate for students' inability to understand science
        texts written for their grade level.

234.   Smith, A. (1980/81). History textbooks for poor
        readers--at what cost? Indiana Social Studies
        Quarterly, 33, 107-115.

        Reports results of a content analysis of the treat-
        ment of the Civil War and the Great Depression in
        seven junior high U.S. history textbooks with reada-
        bility levels below grade seven. The textbooks were
        found to be inadequate in their coverage of the two
        topics in a number of ways, especially failure to
        include historical explanations, cause-effect rela-
        tionships, background material, and overall synthesiz-
        ing information to aid student comprehension.

235.   Spache, G.D. (1964). Estimating readability. In
        Spache, G.D., Good reading for poor readers.
        Champaign, IL: Garrard Publishing Company, 21-28.

        Overviews a variety of topics, including methods of
        estimating readability, agreement among methods of
        estimation, a history of readability formulas,
        applications and limitations of readability formulas,
        and recommendations for use.

236.   Spiegel, D.L., & Wright, J.D. (1983). Biology
        teachers' use of readability concepts when selecting
        texts for students. Journal of Reading, 27, 28-34.

Discusses results of a study in which high school
biology teachers completed a questionnaire to identify
how they selected textbooks to accomodate a wide range
of student reading abilities.

237.   Tierney, R.J., Mosenthal, J., & Kantor, R.N. (1984).
        Classroom applications of text analysis: toward
        improving text selection and use. In Flood, J.
        (Ed.). Promoting reading comprehension. Newark, DE:
        International Reading Association, 139-160.

        Discusses what contributes to or detracts from the
        comprehensibility of text such as whether differences
        exist between the functions a text might serve and the
        purposes for which a text is read; the knowledge re-
        quired to understand a text and the knowlege of the
        reader with whom it is to be used. A framework for
        examining the functions of a text and for comparing
        the purposes and shared experiences of authors and
        readers is posed.

  *   Westbury, I. (1985). Textbook selection. Internation-
        al encyclopedia of education research and studies.
        (Cited above as Item 088.)

238.   Wheeler, G., & Sherman, T.F. (1983). Readability
        formulas revisited. Science and Children, 20(7),
        38-40.

        Describes the methodology of eight popular read-
        ability formulas (Bormuth, Dale-Chall, Flesch, Fry,
        Robert Gunnings Fog Index, Jacobson, SMOG, and Spache)
        and suggests selectors consider readability scores
        along with such factors as content organizations and
        visual aids as indices of student appropriateness.

239.   Wheeler, G., & Sherman, T.F. (1984). A sampling of
        middle school and junior language arts textbooks and
        their readability levels. Reading Improvement, 21,
        191-195.

        Recommends that state departments of education
        require the use of specific formulas and uniform
        presentation of readability results for all texts
        being considered for adoption to avoid having to make
        multiple text comparisons from varying readability
        presentations.

240.   Wright, F.D., & Spiegel, D.L. (1984). How important is
        textbook readability to biology teachers? <u>The
        American Biology Teacher</u>, <u>46</u>, 221-225.

        Discusses the results of a study in which high
        school biology teachers completed a questionnaire
        addressing concerns such as their ability to accurate-
        ly judge the readability level of instructional
        materials, the factors they take into account when
        judging readability levels, and whether they consider
        differences in students' reading ability when choosing
        reading materials.

C. TREATMENT OF WOMEN AND MINORITY GROUPS

241.   Arnold, L. (1975). Marie Curie was great, but...
         School Science and Mathematics, 75, 577-584.
         November.

         Asserts, on the basis of analyses of several high
         school science textbooks, that the view of women
         scientists--and hence of science itself--is woefully
         inadequate. Suggests that an exclusive emphasis on
         individual achievement and past success is misleading
         and that the work of not only women but many non-
         celebrity scientists, including those whose major con-
         tributions are yet to be made, have been neglected in
         science textbooks.

242.   Baskin, B. (1981). The dismal project: the portrayal
         of disability in basal readers. Reading
         Improvement, 18, 42-47.

         Discusses results of an analysis of five basal
         reading series to determine the presence of disabled
         characters. Results indicate that vast improvement is
         needed in textbook information and attitudes regarding
         handicaps and disabilities.

243.   Bordelon, K.W. (1985). Sexism in reading materials.
         The Reading Teacher, 38, 791-797.

         Reviews and discusses studies of the treatment of
         sex roles in reading series published between 1972 and
         1982. While most of the studies indicate "some pro-
         gress in equalization of male-female representation,
         several individual imply that the nature of feminine
         activities did not change substantially." Also
         reviews studies showing student interest in stories
         with males and females in nontraditional roles.

244.   Butterfield, R.A., Demos, E.S., Grant, G.W., Moy,
          P.S., & Perez, A.L. (1979). A multicultural analysis
          of a popular reading series in the International
          Year of the Child. Journal of Negro Education, 48,
          382-389.

          Presents an historical overview of the presentation
          of minority group members in textbooks and discusses
          procedures used by publishers to eliminate bias in
          textbooks. Presents findings of an analysis of the
          1979 Houghton-Mifflin reading series, grades one
          through three, from a "multicultural point of view,
          looking for bias with regard to race, sex, class,
          handicap, and age. Found less bias than in books of
          the sixties and early seventies, but minorities are
          inadequately (often misleadingly) represented.

    *   Ellington, L. (1986). Blacks and Hispanics in high
          school economics texts. Social Education. (Cited
          below as Item 343.)

245.   Fillmer, H.T., & Meadows, R. (1986). The portrayal of
          older characters in five sets of basal readers. The
          Elementary School Journal, 86, 651-662.

          Summarizes previous studies and reports on content
          analysis of all stories, preprimer through grade 6, of
          five basal reading series published between 1975 and
          1983. Found that the proportion of older Americans
          portrayed does not come close to approximating that of
          contemporary society, especially in the ratio of white
          males to females and members of minority groups.
          Discusses implications and includes checklist used in
          analysis.

246.   Garcia, J. (1980). Hispanic perspective: textbooks and
          other curricular materials. The History Teacher,
          13, 105-120.

          Presents results of a content analysis of the
          coverage of Hispanics in 10 secondary U.S. history
          textbooks published in 1978 and 1979. Results of the
          study indicate that textbook writers provide readers
          with limited descriptions mainly of two groups of
          Hispanics--Mexican Americans and Puerto Ricans. These
          descriptions were in most instances slanted and

focused on problems (e.g., unemployment, prejudice, violence, and drugs). Suggests ways for teachers to provide more complete and accurate content.

*   Garcia, J. & Tanner, D.E., The portrayal of black Americans in U.S. history textbooks. The Social Studies. (Cited below as Item 350.)

247.   Garcia, J., & Woodrick, C.S. (1979). The treatment of white and non-white women in U.S. textbooks. The Clearinghouse, 53, 17-22.

Gives results of a content analysis of eight secondary U.S. history textbooks. "The treatment extended to females is, at best, limited." Authors suggest that "there exists a need for accurate, non-balanced, and comprehensive descriptions of white and white females," from all walks of life and involved in a variety of roles.

248.   Grant, C.A., & Grant, G.W. (1981). The multicultural evaluation of some second and third grade textbook readers--a survey analysis. Journal of Negro Education, 50, 63-74.

Reports results of an analysis of three aspects of minority representation in three basal reading programs: diversity (range and variety of character types), setting (time and location of stories, socioeconomic status of characters), and involvement (roles played and degrees of participation). More than half the stories were "all-majority," most depicted the middle class, and white characters most often had the major role, with black characters taking a distant second and other minorities were not as involved in the stories as blacks.

249.   Hahn, C.L., & Blankenship, G. (1981). Women and economics textbooks. Theory and Research in Social Education, 11(3), 67-76.

Reports on study of 21 secondary school textbooks published from 1975 to 1982. Found that these texts were less sex-biased than those examined previously, but that "there is much left to be done to accurately reflect women's economic life," especially their

concentration in low-paying, traditionally female
occupations.

250.   Hopkins, C.J. (1982). Representation of the
        handicapped in basal readers. The Reading Teacher,
        36, 30-32.

        Reports results of a content analysis of all stor-
        ies, preprimer through grade six, in 12 major basal
        reading series. Less than 1% of the stories dealt
        with handicapped characters (almost one-half the
        series contained only one selection), none of these
        stories appeared below grade three, and 25 of the
        total of 39 stories dealt with blindness.
        Implications and recommendations are given.

251.   Kane, M.B. (1970). Minorities in textbooks: a study of
        their treatment in social studies texts. Chicago:
        Anti-Defamation League of B'nai B'rith and Quadrangle
        Books.

        Reports results of a content analysis of 45 second-
        ary U.S. and world history and government and/or soci-
        al problems textbooks published between 1963 and 1969.
        Material on the Jews overemphasizes their ancient past
        and their persecution, Nazi persecutions of minorities
        are still inadequately treated, the black man's strug-
        gle for equality continues to be treated more with
        complacent generalizations than with hard facts, and
        the contemporary role of other minority groups contin-
        ues, for the most part, to be ignored. (See also Item
        254.)

252.   Kirkness, V.J. (1977). Prejudice about Indians in
        textbooks. Journal of Reading, 20, 595-600.

        Summarizes some research findings regarding the
        depiction of Indians in social studies textbooks used
        in Canada. Presents 10 criteria for evaluating text-
        ual materials and suggests that "to get action in
        regard to prejudice in textbooks, it will be necessary
        to act collectively on a national or even internation-
        al basis."

* Krupka, L.R., & Vener, A.M. (1982). Treatment of aging in secondary school biology textbooks: a neglected phenomenon. The American Biology Teacher. (Cited above as Item 321.)

* Kuya, D. (1977). The unacceptable face of publishing. The Times Educational Supplement. (Cited above as Item 130.)

253. Lorimer, R., & Long, M. (1979-80). Sex-role stereotyping in elementary readers. Interchange, 10(2), 25-45.

Summarizes and discusses results of studies of five well-used Canadian reading series. Makes a distinction between sex-role typing and sex-role stereotyping. Concludes that "the general ideology of the readers"--that is, the setting up of a point of view which creates categories of individuals hierarchically related to one another -- "plays the central role, followed by the numerical frequency of characters" in stereotyping.

254. Marcus, L. (1961). Treatment of minorities in secondary school textbooks. New York: Anti-Defamation League of B'nai B'rith.

Reports the findings of a content analysis of 48 U.S. and world history and social-problems textbooks. Treatment of the Jews continues to suffer from over-emphasis on their ancient past and persecution, Nazi persecutions of minority groups are inadequately treated, the Negroes' position in contemporary American society is largely ignored, and immigrants receive considerable attention in U.S. history and social-problems texts. (See also Item 251.)

* Reynolds, C.J. (1952). Textbooks and immigrants. Phi Delta Kappan. (Cited below as Item 370.)

255. Shirreffs, J.H. (1975). Sex-role stereotyping in elementary health education textbooks. Journal of School Health, 45(9), 519-523.

Presents results of a study of five textbook series published from 1969-1974. Found sex-role stereotyping

in all the series, especially on types of activities
in which boys and girls engage, and in the narrow
range of career choices for girls implied in the
illustrations.

256.   Stern, R.H. (1976). Sexism in foreign language
           textbooks. Foreign Language Annals, 9(4), 294-299.

     Reports findings of an analysis of the content and
     photographs of five foreign language textbooks
     published after 1970. The texts "overwhelmingly omit
     women or place them in mundane and eccentric roles."

257.   Trecker, J.L. (1971). Women in U.S. history high
           school textbooks. Social Education, 35, 249-260+.

     Reports results of an examination of 11 textbooks
     and two document collections published between 1957
     and 1968. Found "a curious pattern of inclusions and
     neglects . . . (which) presents the stereotyped
     picture of the American woman--passive, incapable of
     sustained organization or work, satisfied with her
     role in society, and well supplied with material
     blessings."

258.   Westbury, I. (1985). Textbook bias. International
           encyclopedia of education research and studies (Item
           190), 5225-5226.

     Discusses values reflected in textbooks, briefly
     reviews the history of textbook bias and textbook
     revision, and describes the technique of content
     analysis.

259.   Wright, V. (1976-77). Hidden messages: expressions of
           prejudice. Interchange, 7(2), 54-62.

     Presents results of a content analysis of basal
     readers as literature indicating "a striking absence
     of stories plotted and peopled so as to nurture a
     positive self concept in girls" or in any non-white,
     non-Anglo, non-middle class children. Concludes that
     only a "total approach" to the solution of this
     problem will suffice.

IV.   SUBJECT MATTER CONTENT COVERAGE

A. LANGUAGE ARTS

260.   Donsky, B. von B. (1984). Trends in elementary writing instruction, 1900-1959. Language Arts, 61, 795-803.

Describes results of study of learning activities in three representative English language arts textbooks from each of three periods between 1900 and 1969. Found declining trends in the written word and increase in oral language exercises, with grammar and sentence construction remaining essentially unchanged. Discusses the historical trends and the future role of textbooks in writing instruction.

261.   Graves, D.H. (1977). Language arts textbooks: a writing process evaluation. Language Arts, 54, 817-823.

Reports results of analyses of eight language arts textbooks and teacher's editions at both the second- and fifth-grade levels to determine how much and in what way writing was taught. Although writing opportunities are introduced and mechanics emphasized, "the entire (writing) process area is left untouched by the texts." Neither prewriting, composing, or postcomposing activities are "suggested with strength or substance," nor is the learner's capacity for voice development or self-critical capability developed.

*   Jensen, J.M., & Roser, N. (1987). Basal readers and language arts programs. The Elementary School Journal. (Cited as above as Item 010.)

*   Ney, J. (1982). Evaluating the linguistic components of secondary language arts textbooks. English Journal. (Cited above as Item 071.)

*   Wheeler, G., & Sherman, T.F. (1984). A sampling of
middle school and junior high language arts
textbooks and their readability levels. <u>Reading
Improvement</u>. (Cited above as Item 239.)

B. MATHEMATICS

262.   Ballenger, M., Benham, N., & Hosticka, A. (1984).
       Children's counting books: mathematical concept
       development. Childhood Education, 61, 30-35.

       Lists criteria for examining and choosing counting
       books for three- to eight-year-olds, identifies and
       illustrates concept development problems frequently
       found, and presents critiques of 24 counting books
       published between 1946 and 1956.

263.   Callahan, L.G., & Passi, S.L. (1985). Textbooks,
       transitions, and transplants. The Arithmetic
       Teacher, 19, 381-385.

       Presents findings from a study of cognitive process
       levels in grades three to six in three elementary
       textbook series—one published in 1950, two in the
       early 1970s. Found that the textbooks "did not tend
       to foster" higher level cognitive processes. Suggests
       that teachers introduce "well-chosen and appropriate
       laboratory activities" to foster the higher-level pro-
       cesses.

264.   Dooley, M.C. (1960). The relationship between
       arithmetic research and the content of arithmetic
       textbooks: 1900-1957. The Arithmetic Teacher, 7,
       178-183, 188.

       Gives the results of a study of the content of 153
       elementary arithmetic textbook series published be-
       tween 1900 and 1957 to "discover the trends that could
       be found in the acceptance or non-acceptance of re-
       search findings. Reports on topics that apparently
       have (and have not) been influenced by research find-
       ings. Concludes that those recommendations that were
       "clear, concise, and exact" were incorporated into
       many textbooks within five years; lack of clearness
       and explicitness led to slowly developing trends.

*   Feldrake, H.J. (1966). "Student acceptance of the new mathematics programs." The Arithmetic Teacher. (Cited above as Item 159.)

265.   Fey, J.T. (1980). Mathematics teaching today: perspectives from three national studies for the elementary grades. In National Science Foundation (1980). What are the needs in precollege science, mathematics, and social science education? Views from the field (SE 80-9). Washington, D.C.: Author, 33-42.

Summarizes results of three NSF-sponsored studies (Suydam & Osborne, 272; Weiss, 172; and Stake & Easley, 021), including content emphasis and patterns of instructional style and organization.

266.   Freeman, D.J., Kuhs, T.M., Porter, A.C., Floden, R.E., Schmidt, W.H., & Schwille, J.R. (1983). Do textbooks define a national curriculum in elementary school mathematics? The Elementary School Journal, 83, 501-513.

Reports the results of content analyses of four mathematics textbooks and five standardized tests for the fourth grade. Found only a limited number of specific topics emphasized in all the textbooks and tests and concluded that "even the best matched textbooks and tests failed to provide a congruent description of what is taught in fourth-grade mathematics."

267.   Freeman, D.J., Belli, G.M., Porter, A.C., Floden, R.E., Schmidt, W.H., & Schwille, J.R. (1983). The influence of different styles of textbook use on instructional validity of standardized tests. Journal of Educational Measurement, 20, 259-270.

Describes results of a study to determine if the degree of congruity in textbook-test content varies across five different styles of textbook use. Variations were found in content covered on two standardized tests, but not on three others.

268.   Horodezky, B., & Weinstein, P.S. (1981). A comparative
         analysis of vocabulary load of three provincially
         adopted primary arithmetic series. The Alberta
         Journal of Educational Research, 27, 121-132.

         Presents results of a study of the degree of
         variability, overlapping, and vocabulary load in three
         primary arithmetic series. The total number of words
         differed between series and few words were shared in
         common. There was marked increase in different words
         at both second and third grade levels.

269.   Nicely, R.F., Jr. (1985). Higher order thinking in
         mathematics textbooks. Educational Leadership, 42,
         26-30.

         Describes study of cognitive levels in "complex num-
         bers" sections of secondary textbooks printed between
         1961 and 1984 and the "decimals" sections of grades
         three through textbooks printed in the mid-1980s. The
         evidence gathered supports the contention that widely
         used textbooks "rarely pose real problems." Suggests
         staff development focused on the introduction of
         higher-order thinking skills.

270.   Nicely, R.F. (1985). Mathematics instruction: a decade
         of change. International Journal of Instructional
         Media, 12, 127-136.

         Describes the results of applying a system of analy-
         sis to secondary mathematics textbooks published be-
         tween 1961 and 1980. Concluded that, if problem solv-
         ing is to be a major focus of school mathematics dur-
         ing the 1980s, textbooks will be inadequate as (the
         sole) instructional resources to help students acquire
         these higher level cognitive processes.

271.   Saxon, J. (1984). The way we teach our children
         mathematics is a disgrace. American Education,
         20(4), 10-13.

         Argues that the (then) current secondary mathematics
         textbooks are good on introduction of concepts but
         poor when it comes to providing sufficient review and
         practice to insure the mastery of fundamental skills.

272.   Suydam, M.N., & Osborne, A. (1977). The status of pre-
         college science, mathematics, and social science
         education: 1955–1975, Volume II: mathematics educa-
         tion. Columbus: Center for Science and Mathematics
         Education, The Ohio State University, 98–101.

         Summarizes results of three studies of the use of
         textbooks and related materials showing heavy depend-
         ence on them, and several studies of the contents of
         mathematics textbooks indicating greatest emphasis on
         lower-level cognitive processes, agreement on topic
         placement but wide variance in number of concepts
         presented and space devoted to topics, and an emphasis
         on computational skill, among other findings.

C. READING

273.   Anderson, C.W., & Smith, E.L., Children's
        preconceptions and content area textbooks.
        Comprehension instruction (Item 287), 187-201.

        Reports results of astudy of the negative effects of
        fifth-grade students' preconceptions of two topics,
        vision and photosynthesis, on their understanding of
        science instruction. Describes materials designed to
        make children aware of the specific differences
        between their preconceptions and scientific
        conceptions.

274.   Anderson, L., The environment of instruction: the
        function of seatwork in a commercially developed
        curriculum. Comprehension instruction (Item 287),
        93-103.

        Reports on observational study of 32 students in
        eight first-grade classrooms doing seatwork assign-
        ments. Found similarities across classrooms in the
        nature of the work, student understanding of why they
        do the work, and teacher communications about the
        assignments. There was a subgroup of students whose
        responses to seatwork were not facilitative of
        learning and who emphasized completion instead of
        understanding.

275.   Anderson, R.C, Osborn, J., & Tierney, R.J. (Eds.).
        (1984). Learning to read in American schools: basal
        readers and content texts. Hillsdale, NJ: Erlbaum
        Associates.

        (Contains items 211, 276, 280, 283, 288, 301, and
        305.)

282.   Anderson, T.H., & Armbruster, B.B., Content area
         textbooks. <u>Learning to read in American schools:
         basal readers and content texts</u> (Item 275),
         193-226.

         Describes analytic tools used to identify aspects of
         textbook prose that can pose comprehension and learn-
         ing difficulties. Discusses and illustrates four as-
         pects of "considerate" text: structure, coherence,
         unity, and audience appropriateness. Suggests guide-
         lines and a checklist for textbooks authors and
         selectors.

   *   Armbruster, B. B., The problem of "inconsiderate
         text." <u>Comprehension instruction</u>. (Cited above as
         Item 203.)

283.   Armbruster, B.B., & Gudbrandsen, B. (1986). Reading
         comprehension instruction in the social studies.
         <u>Social Studies</u>, <u>21</u>, 36-48.

         Reports on examination of five social studies pro-
         grams at the fourth- and sixth-grade levels to deter-
         mine the amount and kind of reading comprehension
         instruction in student textbooks and teachers'
         editions. Direct instruction in skills was rare and
         there was a great deal of apparent confusion about
         what "reading skills" are and what constitutes a
         legitimate exercise of those skills.

284.   Aukerman, R.C. (1971). <u>Approaches to beginning
         reading</u>. New York: John Wiley & Sons.

         Describes and illustrates the origins and methods
         and materials of some 101 approaches, together with
         summary discussions of the significant contribution
         of each approach to beginning reading and a
         summarization of some definitive research studies.

285.   Beck, I.L., & McKeown, M.G. (1984). Application of
         theories of reading to instruction. <u>American Journal
         of Education</u>, <u>93</u>, 61-81.

         Discusses the application of theory to reading in-
         struction. Summarizes theory and research pertaining
         to background knowledge and its application and text

organization and the creation of more comprehensible
texts. Offers recommendations on both background
knowledge and text organization.

280.   Beck, I.L., Developing comprehension: the impact of
         directed reading lessons. <u>Learning to Read in
         American Schools: Basal Readers and Content Texts</u>
         (Item 275), 3-20.

         Discusses seven issues arising from the analysis of
         directed reading lessons on comprehension in 13 basal
         reading series and makes recommendations. The issues
         were: limited vocabulary in early readers, excessive
         stylization and fit in pictures, divisions within
         stories, connecting with children's prior knowledge,
         handling of new vocabulary, the setting of purpose for
         reading, and after-reading questions.

281.   Bohning, G. (1986). The McGuffey Eclectic Readers:
         1836-1986. <u>The Reading Teacher</u>, <u>40</u>, 263-269.

         Presents an overview of the development and history
         of the McGuffey Readers and discusses their influence
         on current basal series.

282.   Bond, G.L., & Dykstra, R. (1967). The Cooperative
         Research Program in first-grade reading instruction.
         <u>Reading Research Quarterly</u>, <u>2</u>, 5-142.

         Summarizes and discusses the findings of some 27
         studies of the relationships between various
         approaches to beginning reading instruction and
         student achievement in reading. No statistically
         significant differences were found across approaches.
         Concluded that, to improve reading instruction, "it is
         necessary to train better teachers rather than to
         expect a panacea in the form of materials."

  *   Bordelon, K.W. (1985). Sexism in reading materials.
         <u>The Reading Teacher</u>. (Cited above as Item 243.)

283.   Bruce, B., A new point of view on children's stories.
         <u>Learning to read in American schools: basal readers
         and content texts</u> (Item 275), 153-174.

Presents results of study of the variation in
conflict, inside view, and point of view in children's
stories in 200 basal reading texts and children's
tradebooks. Results support the hypothesis that part
of the difficulty children encounter in making the
transition from beginning to skilled reading lies in a
abrupt shift in text characteristics from lower to
upper elementary school. Moreover, the school texts
may provide inadequate preparation for the trade books
and other texts that skilled readers have to master.

*   Butterfield, R.A., Demos, E.S., Grant, G.W., Moy,
        P.S., & Perez, A.L. (1979). A multicultural analysis
        of a popular reading series in the International
        Year of the Child. Journal of Negro Education.
        (Cited above as Item 244.)

284.   Chall, J.S. (1967). A look at the basal-reading
        series. Learning to read: the great debate. New
        York: McGraw-Hill, 200-257.

Reports on descriptive analyses of a sampling of
reading programs. Two widely used traditional basal
reading series contain lessons built around stories,
word method, an emphasis on comprehension, little
phonics or writing, and heavy dependence on the teacher. One newer series that begins with phonics contains lessons built around phonic elements, greater
variety in teaching new words, and similar emphasis on
comprehension. Also describes trends in the Scott,
Foresman programs from 1920 to 1962, including a
decrease in vocabulary load, more space given to
illustrations, and a growth in the teacher's manuals
along with the number of teaching suggestions and
teacher load.

285.   Chall, J.S., & Conard, S.S. (1984). Resources and
        their use for reading instruction. In Purves, A.C.,
        & Niles, O. (Eds.). Becoming a reader in a complex
        society, 83rd Yearbook of the National Society for
        the Study of Education, Part I. Chicago: University
        of Chicago Press, 209-232.

Describes major characteristics of materials for
reading instruction (basal programs, textbooks for
middle and upper grades, content textbooks, trade

books and periodicals) and discusses changes that have
occured over time. Also discusses evaluation and
selection of materials, including readability, fair
representation, and censorship.

286.   Drum, P.A. (1984). Children's understanding of
         passages. In Flood, J. (Ed.). Promoting reading
         comprehension. Newark, Delaware: International
         Reading Association, 61-78.

         Summarizes the results of research on children's
         comprehension of extended language passages and dis-
         cusses possible educational implications. Included
         are the effects of age, of ability levels, of differ-
         ent tasks, and of passage characteristics. Author's
         intent is "to determine what activities children can
         reasonably be expected to perform as a result of
         exposure to passages."

287.   Duffey, G.G., Roehler, L.R., & Mason, J. (1984).
         Comprehension instruction: perspectives and
         suggestions. New York: Longman.

         Contains Items 203, 273, and 274.

  *   Duffey, G. G., Roehler, L. R., & Putnam, J. (1987).
         Putting the teacher in control: basal reading
         textbooks and instructional decision making. The
         Elementary School Journal. (Cited above as Item
         006.)

288.   Durkin, D., Do basal reader manuals provide for read-
         ing comprehension instruction? Learning to read in
         American schools: basal readers and content texts
         (Item 275), 29-38.

         Reports on the analysis of the manuals from five K-6
         basal reading programs. Looked at provisions for in-
         struction, review, application, and practice. Con-
         cluded that manuals had tendency to "offer precise
         help when it is least needed, but they are obscure or
         silent when specific help is likely to be required.
         Even some specific help is of questionable value.

*   Durkin, D. (1987). Influences on basal reading
        programs. The Elementary School Journal (Cited
        above as Item 040.)

289.   Durkin, D. (1981). Reading comprehension instruction
        in five basal reader series. Reading Research
        Quarterly, 16, 515-544.

        Summarizes a study of the suggestions for compre-
        hension instruction in the manuals of five basal read-
        er programs, kindergarten through grade six. The
        study found that the manuals give far more attention
        to assessment and practice than to direct, explicit
        instruction. When provisions for teaching children
        how to comprehend are provided, they tend to be brief.
        These findings are related to an earlier classroom-
        observation study, similarities in the findings of the
        two studies are discussed and recommendations made for
        change in the teaching guides.

290.   Durkin, D. (1974). Some questions about questionable
        instructional materials. The Reading Teacher, 28,
        13-17.

        Describes and illustrates two findings that emerged
        from classroom observation of the teaching of reading:
        teachers spending time on unnecessary and even errone-
        ous instruction that was often the result of unques-
        tioning use of basal reader manuals and basal reader
        and other workbooks. Stresses need for teachers who
        are both willing and able to assume truly professional
        roles and thus make decisions about what will be
        taught, how it will be taught, and to whom.

291.   Educational Products Information Exchange Institute
        (1982-83). Annual state of the art report on
        instructional materials: reading textbook programs
        (Report No. 100m). New York: Author.

        After giving a comparative overview of the basal
        programs then on the market and presenting an annotat-
        ed listing of 28 years of key professional publica-
        tions on the improvement of reading instruction, pre-
        sents an analysis of provisions for the teaching of
        phonics and comprehension in a selection of major
        basal reading series.

292.   Flesch, R. (1955). <u>Why Johnny can't read, and what you</u>
         <u>can do about it.</u> New York: Harper & Row.

         Argues that, if the "look-and-say" method could just
         be replaced by the "phonics-first" method in the
         teaching of beginning reading, the reading problem
         would be solved.

293.   Flesch, R. (1981). <u>Why Johnny still can't read.</u> New
         York: Harper & Row.

         Distinguishes between the "dismal dozen" basal
         reading series and the "phonics five" on the basis of
         how many of 181 phonic elements are introduced and
         mastered through drill and practice. Estimates that
         only 15% of the nation's students are currently using
         the "phonics five" programs and thus "there's an 85%
         chance that . . . Johnny and Mary will never learn to
         read."

294.   Fry, E., & Sakley, E. (1986). Common words not taught
         in basal reading series. <u>The Reading Teacher</u>, <u>39</u>,
         395-398.

         Reports that a study of five major American basal
         reading series found that only from 50% to 59% per
         cent of the 3000 most common English words are
         taught.

295.   Graney, M. (1977). Role models in children's readers.
         <u>School Review,</u> <u>85</u>, 247-63.

         Reports results of a comparative analysis of role
         models in McGuffey's Readers and a sample of nine
         modern readers published before 1970. Findings indi-
         cate shifts from individual to collective authority
         and from inner-directed to other-directed fictional
         characters, but not in the kinds of overt behaviors
         described.

  *   Grant, C.A., & Grant, G.W. (1981). The multicultural
         evaluation of some second and third grade textbook
         readers--a survey analysis. <u>Journal of Negro</u>
         <u>Education.</u> (Cited above as Item 248.)

296.   Green-Wilder, J.L., & Kingston, A.J. (1986). The
          depiction of reading in five popular basal series.
          The Reading Teacher, 39, 399-402.

          Reports results of a content analysis of five basal
          reading series to ascertain the extent to which the
          act of reading is portrayed. Found that an average of
          11% the selections contained reading events, but few
          of these contained "more than fleeting reference to
          reading behaviors," and reading "was not portrayed as
          an integral or important part of daily activities."

297.   Herrick, V.E. (1961). Basal instructional materials in
          reading. In Henry, N.B. (Ed.). Development in and
          through reading, 60th Yearbook of the National
          Society for the Study of Education, Part I.
          Chicago: University of Chicago Press, 165-188.

          Reviews the theoretical considerations involved in
          determining the extent to which a reading material
          could be basal, the nature and range of present read-
          ing materials considered as basal, and the reported
          research on the extent of the use and comparative
          evaluations of such materials. Draws conclusions
          regarding the characteristics of basal reading materi-
          als, the range of materials and instructional settings
          required for effective instruction, the need to im-
          prove teaching method and over-all instructional plan-
          ning, and the failure of research to demonstrate the
          superiority of any one method or set of materials.

298.   Hoffman, J.V. (1987). Rethinking the role of oral
          reading in basal instruction. The Elementary School
          Journal, 87, 367-373.

          Reports findings from a study of reading instruction
          for low-ability basal reading groups that offers an
          emphasis on comprehension and fluent, expressive
          reading as an alternative to the practice recommended
          by the publishers of basal series.

   *   Hopkins, C.J. (1982). The representation of the handi-
          capped in basal readers. The Reading Teacher.
          (Cited above as Item 250.)

*   Jensen, J. M., & Roser, N. (1987). Basal readers and
        language arts programs. The Elementary School
        Journal, 87, 375-383. (Cited above as Item 010.)

299.   Juel, C., & Roper/Schneider, D. (1985). The influence
        of basal readers on first grade reading. Reading
        Research Quarterly, 20, 134-152.

        Reports results of a study of the role of various
        word features and basal text factors in the developing
        word recognition skills of 93 first-grade students.
        The relative influence of the word characteristics in
        two different types of basal readers on the acquisi-
        tion of word identification skills was evaluated sev-
        eral times during the first-grade year. Results indi-
        cate that the text children are exposed to early in
        first grade may differentially shape their word iden-
        tification strategies.

*   Mason, J.M. (1983). An examination of reading
        instruction in third and fourth grades. The Reading
        Teacher. (Cited above as Item 012.)

300.   Osborn, J.H., Jones, B.F., & Stein, M. (1985). The
        case for improving textbooks. Educational
        Leadership, 42, 9-16.

        Synthesizes and discusses 10 years of research on
        text and textbooks under the headings of relevant
        research findings (schema and metacognitive theories
        and instructional design), "considerateness" (text
        structure, coherence, unity and audience appropriate-
        ness), and analysis of existing textbooks (readability
        formulas, basal reader narratives, vocabulary texts,
        teachers' manuals, student practice materials).

301.   Osborn, J. The purposes, uses and contents of
        workbooks and some guidelines for publishers.
        Learning to read in American schools: basal readers
        and content texts (Item 275), 45-110.

        Discusses and critiques the role of reading work-
        books in elementary classrooms. Describes how work-
        books serve teachers and students and summarizes a
        study of their use in classrooms. Suggests implica-
        tions for developers of basal programs, including 20

guidelines for workbook tasks. Illustrates descriptions, critiques, and guidelines with examples of workbook pages.

302.   Seymour, C.R., Palmatier, R.A., Dulaney, K.H., &
         Bailey, M.H. (1983-84). Vocabulary load in basal
         reader workbooks. Reading Improvement, 20, 295-298.

    Reports results of the examination of workbooks from
three mid-1970s basal reading programs for grade 1-3
to determine the incidence of new vocabulary words
appearing in the workbooks. All except one book were
found to contain at least 30 per cent new vocabulary
items not introduced at previous levels or at the
level for which the workbook was designed. Results
indicate that teachers must not expect independent use
of workbooks by students.

303.   Shannon, P. (1983). The treatment of commercial
         reading materials in college reading methods
         textbooks. Reading World, 23, 146-157.

    Reports results of analysis of six randomly selected
reading methods textbooks to determine the authors'
perspectives on commercial reading materials and their
use in elementary classrooms. Found highly similar
characterizations across authors and concluded that
authors are relatively uncritical in the advocacy of
commercial materials and their use.

  *   Shannon, P. (1983). The use of commercial reading
         materials in American elementary schools. Reading
         Research Quarterly. (Cited above as Item 020.)

304.   Templeton, S. (1986). Literacy, readiness, and
         basals. The Reading Teacher, 39, 403-409.

    Reviews recent research findings and implications
regarding beginning literacy: its social context, the
development of a meta-language, and the conventions of
printed language. Presents examples from activities
from basal reading series intended for readiness and
beginning reading that "should be avoided or, at least
for many children, postponed."

305.   Tierney, R.J. A synthesis of research on the use of
         instructional texts: some implications for the
         educational publishing industry in reading."
         Learning to read in American schools: basal readers
         and content texts (Item 275), 287-296.

             Summarizes three recurring themes emanating from the
         1981 Tarrytown Conference and suggests how these
         themes apply to basal and textbook development and to
         directions for future research. The themes deal with:
         (a) the quality of text material and criteria for text
         selection, (b) the shortcomings of the present compre-
         hension curricula and skill objectives, and (c) the
         dearth of teaching procedures for the improvement of
         reading comprehension.

    *   Venezky, R.L. (1987). A history of the American
         reading textbook. The Elementary School Journal.
         (Cited above as Item 022.)

306.   Wargny, F.O. (1963). The good life in modern readers.
         The Reading Teacher, 17, 88-93.

             Reviews a study comparing how topics such as race,
         family relations, and social problems were treated in
         431 stories appearing in various modern reading series
         and compares their treatment in 151 stories in a
         series of McGuffey's Readers. The purpose of the
         study was to determine how the good life was depicted
         in modern reading texts and what courses of action,
         conditions, and elements of experience seem to be pre-
         ferred by the authors of these texts.

    *   Wilson, A.H. (1980). The image of Africa in elementary
         schools. Social Education. (Cited below as Item
         377).

    *   Wilson, C.A., & Hammill, C. (1982). Inferencing and
         comprehension in ninth graders reading geography
         textbooks. Journal of Reading. (Cited below as
         Item 378.)

307.   Winograd, P., & Greenlee, M. (1986). Students need a
         balanced reading program. Educational Leadership,
         43, 16-21.

Reviews and synthesizes research studies in comparing "reductionist" and "strategic" approaches to reading instruction. Argues for a balanced approach that requires intentionality, interest, and motivation on the part of the learner rather than exclusive emphasis on learning subskills and passing achievement test items.

*   Wright, V. (1976-77). Hidden messages: expressions of prejudice. _Interchange_. (Cited above as Item 259.)

*   Zimet, S.F. (1969). American elementary reading textbooks: a sociological review. _Teachers College Record_. (Cited below as Item 392).

D. SCIENCE

* Arnold, L. (1975). Marie Curie was great, but...
   School Science and Mathematics. (Cited above as
   Item 241.)

* Anderson, C.W., & Smith, E.L. (1984). Children's pre-
   conceptions and content area textbooks. Comprehension instruction. (Cited above as Item 273.)

308. Babikian, E. (1975). An aberrated image of science in
      elementary school science textbooks. School Science
      and Mathematics, 75, 457-462.

      Reports results of a content analysis of six elemen-
      tary science textbook series and an opinion survey of
      549 students from grades two, four, and six. Found
      that questions posed and experiments provided have ex-
      plicit answers or outcomes, but the answers or out-
      comes for most of them are withheld. Unanswerable
      questions and unexplorable experiments are not includ-
      ed. Thus these textbooks do not reflect the true
      nature of science.

309. Barrass, R. (1984). Some misconceptions and
      misunderstandings perpetuated by teachers and
      textbooks of biology. Journal of Biological
      Education, 18(3), 201-205.

      Presents an "annotated list of some misconceptions
      and misunderstandings commonly encountered in the
      written work of students who have passed their school
      examinations in biology." Discusses the reasons why
      teachers and textbooks of biology "continue to teach
      things that are known to be incorrect."

310. Brody, P.J. (1982-83). An analysis of pictures in
      middle level life science textbooks. International
      Journal of Instructional Media, 10(2), 113-121.

Reports on a study to determine if five representative middle level life science textbooks used pictures
in a manner consistent with criteria which have been
shown to increase the instructional effectiveness of
pictures. The results indicate that the pictures do
not always meet appropriate criteria.

311.   Carrick, T. (1977). A comparison of recently published
         biology textbooks for first examinations. Journal
         of Biological Education, 11(3), 163-175.

Describes the characteristics of recently published
textbooks, comparing aims, content, methods of presentation, and the ways questions are employed. Shows
that a wide range of approaches to the teaching of
biology are represented.

312.   Curtis, R.V., & Reigeluth, C.M. (1984). The use of
         analogies in written text. Instructional Science,
         13, 99-117.

Summarizes an investigation in the use of analogies
in the design of 26 science textbooks, ranging from
elementary to post-secondary. A total of 216 analogies were identified and classified and a set of prescriptions regarding the use of analogies in written
instruction are proposed.

313.   Denny, M. (1983). Children's perception of science: an
         analysis of the notion of infallibility in the
         coverage of evolution in 'textbooks' and some other
         teaching materials. Educational Studies, 9(2),
         93-103.

Argues that the authority of the printed word in
textbooks plays a major role in influencing children
in their beliefs and attitudes about science and that
textbooks provide an image of science that is "totally
inconsistent with the actual nature of science"; i.e.,
that it is infallible. Illustrates with statements on
evolution from textbooks.

314.   DeRose, J.V., Lockard, J.D., & Paldy, L.G. (1979).
         Teacher is the key: report on three NSF studies.
         The Science Teacher, 46(4), 31-37.

Summarizes results of three studies (see Weiss, 172; Helgeson et al., 318; and Stake & Easley, 021) on patterns of instruction, including the use of textbooks and other materials.

315.   Duschl, R. (1986). Textbooks and the teaching of fluid inquiry. School Science and Mathematics, 86, 27-32.

Proposes that Schwab's idea of pre-college science as "fluid" (as opposed to "stable") inquiry--or inquiry into inquiry--be implemented through the use of textbooks that span 50 to 100 years of publication dates to assist students and teachers to learn about and to teach about the "nature of scientific knowledge that forms the historical development of science."

316.   Elliott, D.L., & Nagel, K.C. (1987). School science and the pursuit of knowledge--deadends and all. Science and Children, 24(8), 9-12.

Reports that an examination of nine elementary science series published between 1984 and 1986 emphasize the products of science (through topic coverage, memorization of content, and cookbook-style hands-on activities with predetermined results) rather than the process. Suggests ways in which the textbook can be supplemented to take students beyond the pursuit of the known.

317.   Gabel, D.E. (1983). What high school chemistry texts do well and what they do poorly. Journal of Chemical Education, 60, 893-895.

Praises publishers for making frequent revision of textbooks to include updated, scientifically correct information. Discusses problems involved in adding new material (e.g., the problem of superficiality if material is condensed) and in the stress on memorization rather than understanding. Suggests teachers insist that publishers implement NSTA "cluster goals."

318.   Helgeson, S.L., Blosser, P.E., & Howe, R.W. (1977).
        The status of pre-college science, mathematics, and
        social science education, Volume I: science
        education. Columbus: Center for Science and
        Mathematics Education, The Ohio State University,
        16-37.

        Summarizes reports on elementary and secondary
        science programs, including instructional practices,
        the use of textbooks, the influence of NSF-sponsored
        "new science" projects, enrollment in secondary
        science courses, and the impact of state textbook
        adoptions.

319.   Hurd, P.DeH., Bybee, R.W., Kahle, J.B., & Yager, R.E.
        (1980). Biology education in secondary schools of
        the United States. The American Biology Teacher,
        42, 388-410.

        Presents a prospective synthesis of sources of in-
        formation presently influencing biology teaching.
        Concludes that "the goals of biology education"--i.e.,
        of textbooks in biology--"are not relevant to present
        priorities in science and society" because the goals
        of biological knowledge, scientific methods, social
        issues, personal needs, and career awareness need to
        be updated.

320.   Koval, D.B., & Staver, J.R. (1985). What textbooks
        don't teach. The Science Teacher, 52(3), 49-52.

        Describes a study which uses comparative frequencies
        with which categories of scientific terms occur in
        high school and junior college physical science texts
        to show that high school courses do not prepare
        students for training as technicians in community
        colleges and other postsecondary technical-training
        institutions.

321.   Krupka, L.R., & Vener, A.M. (1982). Treatment of aging
        in secondary school biology textbooks: a neglected
        phenomenon. The American Biology Teacher, 44,
        264-269.

        Reports on the results of a survey regarding the
        extent of coverage of the aging process in 38 biology

textbooks published from 1966 to 1981. "A general
lack of information with respect to both aging and
senescence was apparent." 32 texts did not include
any material and no text was judged to be adequate in
dealing with the aging process. Implications are
discussed and recommendations made.

322.   Lehrman, R.L. (1982). Confused physics: a tutorial
        critique. The Physics Teacher, 20, 519-523.

        Reports on the errors found in an examination of 14
        high school physics textbooks published between 1970
        and 1982. Suggests two sources of errors: a)
        "careless and non-analytic acceptance of ideas that
        have passed on from textbook to textbook" and b) "a
        specific deficiency in the author's knowledge of his
        subject."

323.   Lowery, L.F., & Leonard, W.H. (1978). A comparison of
        questioning styles among four widely used high
        school biology textbooks. Journal of Research in
        Science Teaching, 15, 1-10.

        Reports significant differences in the ratio of
        questions to sentences per page and notable differ-
        ences in the frequency and position of questions tal-
        lied into the question categories of rhetorical,
        direct information, focusing, open-ended, and valuing.
        Discusses implications regarding the use of "higher
        order" questions and the teaching of inquiry.

324.   Newton, D.P. (1983). The sixth-form physics textbook,
        1870-1980--Part 2. Physics Education, 18(5),
        240-246.

        Summarizes the results of a study of the exposition-
        al content of 35 textbooks under categories labeled
        aims, teaching methods, cognitive and general, affec-
        tive and conative, incidental component, instances and
        exemplars, and genealogical relationships. Also dis-
        cusses factors influencing the writing of physics
        textbooks.

325.   Pauling, L. (1983). Throwing the book at elementary
        chemistry. The Science Teacher, 50, 25-29.
        September.

Discusses and illustrates problems he found with
high school chemistry textbooks: too much information
presented at too advanced a level, errors, and the
inclusion of complex and confusing topics (e.g.,
molecular orbitals).

326.   Pratt, D.L. (1985). Mathematics usage in secondary
        science courses and textbooks. School Science and
        Mathematics, 85, 394-406.

Reviews selected literature on the integration of
science and mathematics instruction. Reports on study
of trends in 26 science textbooks published in the
period 1963-1982 that found: a decrease of mathematics
emphasis in non-traditional chemistry and earth science, no need for advanced mathematics in physics, and
too little attention to problem solving with a mathe-
matical emphasis.

327.   Rigden, J.S. (1983). The art of great science. Phi
        Delta Kappan, 64, 613-617.

Criticizes textbooks as a major source of a common
view that advances in science do not depend on
inspiration and imagination but come (only) from
straightforward logical thinking that is not only
"smooth and unerring" but "routine and inevitable."
"Scientific knowledge is the overriding concern of
textbook writers; the quest for that knowledge is
ignored."

328.   Rosenthal, D.B. (1984). Social issues in high school
        biology textbooks: 1963-1983. Journal of Research
        in Science Teaching, 21, 819-831.

Summarizes and discusses results of an analysis of
of the social issues content of 22 high school biology
textbooks published between 1963 and 1983. Found that
the percentage of total text devoted to 12 categories
of social issues has declined and the treatment of
science and society minimizes the controversial aspects, avoids questions of ethics and values, lacks
global perspective, and neglects the interdisciplinary
nature of problems. Discusses implications.

329.   Stuart, J.A. (1982). An identification of life science
         concepts in selected secondary school science
         textbooks. School Science and Mathematics, 82,
         189-200.

         Reports results of a content analysis of 15 text-
         books to identify the concepts included from six major
         concept areas: physiology, morphology, genetics, evo-
         lution, ecology, applied biology. Found considerable
         agreement in the percentages of total concepts for
         each of the major areas.

330.   Tamir, P., & Lunetta, V.N. (1978). An analysis of
         laboratory inquiries in the BSCS Yellow Version.
         The American Biology Teacher, 40, 353-357.

         Describes a "more refined scheme" for analyzing
         laboratory investigations, uses the scheme to analyze
         the Third Edition of the BSCS Yellow Version, and dis-
         cusses implications of this analysis for instruction
         and curriculum development.

331.   Vanek, E.P., & Montean, J.J. (1977). The effect of two
         science programs (ESS and Laidlaw) on student
         classification skills, science achievement, and
         attitudes. Journal of Research in Science Teaching,
         14, 57-62.

         Describes a study comparing the effects on third-
         and fourth-graders ESS (1966-71) and Laidlaw Science
         series (1966); no measure of actual differences in
         treatment was made. Found that neither teaching meth-
         od nor materials make any apparent difference on the
         student outcomes measured and concluded that "the as-
         sumptions that ESS differs from the textbook classroom
         are not substantiated."

332.   Yager, R.E. (1983). The importance of terminology in
         teaching K-12 science. Journal of Research in
         Science Teaching, 20, 577-588.

         Reports results of analyses of 25 of the most com-
         monly used textbooks in terms of the occurence of
         special/technical works. The number of words intro-
         duced at each level approaches the expected total
         vocabulary increase per student per grade level.

There is evidence that a major aspect of the current
crisis in science education "is the considerable
emphasis on words/terms/definitions as the primary
ingredient of science."

E. SOCIAL STUDIES

333.   Agostino, V.R., & Barone, W.P. (1985). A decade of
         change: elementary social studies texts. Social
         Studies Journal, 14, 20-29.

         Reports on a comparative study of selected social
         studies textbook programs published in the late 1970s
         and early 1980s with those published a decade earlier.
         Reports that few of the "new social studies" innova-
         tions of the earlier programs found their way into
         those published later.

334.   Anderson, N., & Beck, R. (1983). Central America by
         the book: what children are learning. Social
         Education, 47, 102-109.

         Gives results of a critique of the presentation of
         Central American countries in world history and world
         geography textbooks (1977-1982) and other school books
         (1960-1982) by expert reviewers. Findings indicate
         books show that Central American countries are import-
         ant only insofar as they affect U.S. interests; these
         countries are underdeveloped and either tranquil back-
         waters or trouble-torn areas and their people are "not
         like us."

335.   Anyon, J. (1979). Ideology and United States history
         textbooks. Harvard Educational Review, 49, 361-
         386.

         Reports the findings of a content analysis of 17
         widely used secondary school U.S. history textbooks
         published between 1972 and 1979, focusing on economic
         and labor history from 1865 to 1917. Found that the
         content of the textbooks reflects an ideology that
         serves the interests of particular groups (e.g., in-
         dustrialists, inventors) to the exclusion of others
         (e.g., labor, the poor, minorities, women).

*   Armbruster, B.B., & Gudbrandsen, B. (1986). Reading
        comprehension instruction in the social studies.
        Social Studies. (Cited above as 277.)

336.   Barger, H.M. (1976). Demythologizing the textbook
        president: teaching about the president after
        Watergate. Theory and Research in Social Education,
        4(1), 51-66.

        Reviews six American Government textbooks published
        between 1964 and 1972 focusing on their treatment of
        the presidency, with particular emphasis on the degree
        to which they differentiate the presidency in terms of
        regime, incumbent, and our political system. Includes
        results of surveys of the attitudes of samples of ele-
        mentary and secondary students towards the president.

337.   Becker, J. (1981). The Japan/United States Textbook
        Study Project: in search of mutual understanding.
        Social Education, 46, 494-497.

        Summarizes the results of a joint study of social
        studies textbooks by Japanese and American educators.
        Found that "the basic learning material used by youth
        in their respective countries carried messages and
        created images that were inaccurate, biased, or incom-
        plete." Recommends improving the quality of textbooks
        in both countries.

338.   Birchall, G., & Faichney, G. (1985). Images of
        Australia in elementary social studies texts. The
        Social Studies, 76, 120-124.

        Desribes a content analysis study of information
        about Australia in seven elementary school social
        studies textbook series published between 1980 and
        1982. References to Australia ranged from 0.3% to 5%
        of total content and covered geography, rural indus-
        try, aboriginal culture, history of the original Eng-
        lish settlement, and some aspects of urban living.
        The information was generally accurate, but consti-
        tuted an incomplete picture of life in modern
        Australia.

339.   Carroll, J.D., Broadnax, W.D.,, Contreras, G., Mann,
         T.E., Ornstein, N.J., & Stiehm, J. (1987). We the
         people: a review of U.S. government and civics
         textbooks. Washington, D.C.: People for the
         American Way.

         Reports results of an examination of 13 commonly
         used textbooks. Found the textbooks encyclopedic and
         comprehensive in scope, with too much stress on facts
         and too little on concepts, methods, or critical
         thinking about American public values, the conflicts
         among them, and the necessity for continually making
         choices. A number of recommendations are made.

340.   Crutcher, A. Government as social worker. Values in
         an American government textbook (Item 361), 28-38.

         Describes American Government in Action as a "gen-
         erally competent textbook . . . marred chiefly, where
         it is flawed, by superficiality and a tendency to be
         banal. The impulse to liberal trendiness is there,
         but it is restrained by a preternatural cautiousness.
         Details a number of strengths and weaknesses of the
         book.

341.   Danilov, A.I., & Sharifzhanov, I.I. (1961). The
         history of the USSR according to school textbooks of
         the USA. Social Education, 45, 239-244.

         Describes findings of Russian reviewers regarding
         the treatment of Russian history in selected world
         history textbooks published in the 1970s in the United
         States. The books have made marked progress compared
         to analogous textbooks from the 1950s and 1960s, but
         they are "by no means free of the legacy of the Cold
         War and the typical features of their treatment of
         Russian and Soviet history remain as before: political
         bias, oversimplification, and distortion of the
         truth." Examples of these problems are given.

342.   Downey, M.T. (1980). Speaking of textbooks: putting
         pressure on the publishers. The History Teacher,
         14, 61-72.

         Suggests that one reason for the poor quality of
         secondary U.S. history textbooks is that the scholarly

community has not taken an active interest in them. Asserts that U.S. history textbooks ought to be reviewed more regularly and suggests minimal criteria to apply in such reviews. Illustrates the use of these criteria by writing a "trial run of a textbook review" of the 1977 edition of the Todd and Curti Rise of the American Nation.

343. Ellington, L. (1986). Blacks and Hispanics in high school economics texts. Social Education (Item 373), 64-67.

Reports results of a content analysis of 12 secondary economics textbooks published between 1980 and 1985 to assess treatment of the topics of poverty, unemployment, and labor issues. Found that the treatment of blacks and Hispanics was almost entirely descriptive, with only half including data on poverty and only a third including data on unemployment for these two groups.

344. Elliott, D.L., Nagel, K.C., & Woodward, A. (1985). Do textbooks belong in elementary social studies? Educational Leadership, 42, 22-25.

Reports on an instructional design analysis of ten K-6 social studies basal textbook programs. Six common traits were found: a) the series consisted of loosely related collections of separate grade level texts, b) the study of U.S. history dominated, c) most series were similar in content, methodology, scope and sequence, d) many topics were covered only superficially, e) representations of women and minority group members were unrealistic, and f) skill strands emphasized map and globe skills. Recommends that teachers develop alternative resources rather than relying on textbooks to fulfill social studies goals.

345. English, R. (1986). Can social studies textbooks have scholarly integrity? Social Education (Item 373), 46-48.

Argues that, because of the system for textbook production and adoption, "integrity in the search for truth is not the aim of the textbook business." Pressures on publishers from various political groups (and

use of readability formulas) results in "monotony,
sameness, blandness, glossiness, a vapid style and an
elusive quality that makes young readers despise and
hate" textbooks. Calls for more choice and competition in the textbook business.

*   Fetsko, W. (1979). Textbooks and the new social
      studies. The Social Studies. (Cited above as Item
      160.)

346.   Fitzgerald, F. (1979). America revised: history
        schoolbooks in the twentieth century. Boston:
        Little, Brown.

        Presents the result of a comprehensive study of ju-
        nior and senior high school U.S. history textbooks
        published since 1900. Found that pedagogical fads,
        political interest groups influences, and other preju-
        dices of the time have led to the revising of history to
        reflect current values--thus losing continuity and
        precluding generations of students from sharing any
        common reading of the past. Today's textbooks are
        written by committees and designed to be simplistic
        and to offend no one, making them incredibly dull.
        True scholars have little or no role (or interest) in
        the writing of textbooks any longer. (See also Items
        095 and 131.)

347.   Fleming, D. (1981). The impact of nationalism on world
        geography textbooks in the United States.
        International Journal of Political Education, 5(4),
        373-381.

        Summarizes results of previous studies of the influ-
        ence of nationalism in textbooks in history, geogra-
        phy, government and economics. Reports results of an
        analysis of six world geography textbooks (copyright
        1975-1979). Specific examples of nationalistic bias
        are cited and particular emphasis is given to the
        parallel between changes in American foreign policy
        and the focus of textbook content.

348.   Fleming, D.B., & Nurse, R.J. (1982). Vietnam revised:
        are our textbooks changing? Social Education, 46,
        338-343.

Reports on an evaluation of the coverage of the
Vietnam War in 10 secondary level U.S. history textbooks published between 1977 and 1981. The 10 textbook narratives tend to focus primarily on the political and military aspects of the war with more even-
handedness, and with less nationalistic bias, than
those published in the 1960s and early 1970s. Most
textbooks offer too sketchy an account of the war, but
the deficiencies are due to the neglect of certain key
topics rather than distortion, dishonesty, inaccuracy,
or bias.

*   Garcia, J. (1980). Hispanic perspective: textbooks and
        other curricular materials. The History Teacher.
        (Cited above as Item 246.)

349.   Garcia, J. (1986). The white ethnic experience in
        selected secondary U.S. history textbooks. The
        Social Studies, 77, 169-175.

Reports results of a comparative study of the treatment of Irish, Italian, Jewish, and Polish Americans
in secondary social studies textbooks published during
three periods: 1956-75, 1977-78, and 1984-86. Found
the quantitative coverage varied from one period to
another. The qualitative treatment does not differ,
however, and continues to portray the groups collec-
tively in a manner that reflects the melting-pot
ideology.

350.   Garcia, J., & Tanner, D.E. (1985). The portrayal of
        black Americans in U.S. history textbooks. The
        Social Studies, 76, 200-204.

Reviews and critiques some previous studies and reports on analysis of 11 secondary U.S. history textbooks published in 1983 and 1984. Found average of
one sentence per page devoted to the black experience,
but these sentences were unevenly distributed. This
is said to be an improvement over previous editions,
but some important questions were left unaddressed
(e.g., experiences of blacks and whites during the
colonial period and the effects of racism on both
groups).

351.   Goodman, G., Homma, N., Najita, T., & Becker, J.M.
            (1983). The Japan/United States Textbook Project:
            perceptions in the textbooks in each country about
            the history of the other. The History Teacher, 16,
            541-567.

            Becker describes the project in which 14 Japanese
            and 28 American secondary social studies textbooks
            were exchanged and reviewed. Homma summarizes the
            findings that the treatment of Japan in the American
            textbooks was more extensive, more accurate, and less
            biased than in past accounts, although there were
            numerous errors and omissions and too little informa-
            tion on contemporary life in Japan. Najita discusses
            the politics of textbook production in Japan. Becker
            summarizes the Project's general findings and recom-
            mendations for the improvement of textbooks. (See also
            Items 371 and 379.)

   *   Grant, C.A., & Grant, G.W. (1981). The multicultural
            evaluation of some second and third grade textbook
            readers--a survey analysis. Journal of Negro
            Education. (Cited above as Item 248.)

352.   Griffen, W., & Marciano, J. (1980). Vietnam--the
            textbook version. Social Science Record, 17, 16-21.

            Reports on a comparative analysis of the reporting
            of the Vietnam War in a potpourri of 28 high school
            textbooks published between 1961 and 1978 and a "con-
            cise history" of that war based on The Pentagon Papers
            and other government reports. Concludes that the
            textbooks "seem to conspire to construct an environ-
            ment in which the truth is mangled and a whole genera-
            tion deceived" in order to support the official United
            States government policy and omitting varying points
            of view on the war and evidence supporting these
            points of view. Suggests resources for "balancing"
            the textbook accounts.

353.   Gross, R.E. (1952). American history teachers look at
            the book. Phi Delta Kappan (Item 193), 290-291.

            Summarizes the results of several surveys of high
            school U.S. history teachers in California. Teachers
            vary as to the kind of basic textbook they prefer, but

most agree that they do not need "more of the catalo-
gic enumerating textbooks which touch everything and
cover nothing."

* Haas, J.D. (1977). <u>The era of the New Social Studies</u>.
  (Cited above as Item 161.)

* Hahn, C.L., & Blankenship, G. (1981). Women and
  economics textbooks. <u>Theory and Research in Social
  Education</u>. (Cited above as Item 249.)

354. Hodenfield, G.K. (1979). U.S.-U.S.S.R. Textbook
     Project. <u>American Education</u>, <u>15</u>(1), 27-29.

     Describes a joint effort in which U.S. and Soviet
     scholars examined each others' textbooks for factual
     errors and ideological distortions that might
     influence how one nation perceives the other.

355. Jackson, R.H. (1976). The persistence of outmoded
     ideas in high school geography texts. <u>The Journal
     of Geography</u>, <u>75</u>, 399-408.

     Reports on the results of the examination of 44 sec-
     ondary level geography texts published from 1900 to
     1970 to determine how long ideas which had been aban-
     doned at the university level persisted. Environment-
     al determinism as the basic explanation of man's
     activities on earth was used as an index of change and
     not until the 1960s did determinism begin to be widely
     questioned in secondary texts--at least 20 years after
     it was abandoned as a central theme at the university
     level. Some reasons for this are suggested.

356. Jacobs, D. (1981). Teaching the Arab world. <u>The
     Social Studies</u>, <u>72</u>, 150-153.

     Reports on a study done by the National Association
     of Arab Americans (NAAA) in which 19 junior and senior
     high school history books were evaluated for their
     coverage of nine Middle East subjects including polit-
     ical factors, religion, Arab characteristics, women,
     and Arab-Israeli conflict. Disappointing results led
     evaluators to make a number of suggestions to teachers
     for evaluating textbook coverage such as checking cur-
     rency of information and use of value-laden language.

357.   Janis, J. (1972). Textbook revisions in the sixties.
        Teachers College Record, 72, 289-301.

        Discusses and illustrates differences in the treat-
        ment of slavery and the Reconstruction Era between
        secondary U.S. history textbooks published in the
        1950s and early 1960s and those published in the
        middle and late 1960s. Those from the latter period
        were revised to reflect the most recent findings of
        modern American historians.

358.   Kealey, R.J. (1980). The image of the family in
        second-grade readers. Momentum, 11, 16-19.

        Describes the results of a study of the image of the
        family as it appears in six second-grade reading ser-
        ies published since 1978. The number of stories
        relating to one of a variety of family situations
        ranged from 35 per cent to almost 98 per cent. Single
        parents, grandparents and other relatives are includ-
        ed, but no mention is made of foster homes, adoption,
        divorce, or death of a parent.

   *   Kirkness, V. J. (1977). Prejudice about Indians in
        textbooks." Journal of Reading. (Cited above as
        Item 252.)

359.   Kirkpatrick, J. The trivialization of government.
        Values in an American government textbook (Item
        361), 17-27.

        Describes American Government in Action, as a "bet-
        ter introduction to American government than are many
        college textbooks I have read," but cites and docu-
        ments three shortcomings: dullness, intellectual slop-
        piness, and failure to communicate the basic values of
        the American tradition.

360.   Kretman, K.P., & Parker, B. (1986). New U.S. history
        textbooks: good news and bad. Social Education, 50,
        61-63.

        Summarizes the textbook review criteria developed by
        a People for The American Way panel and the findings
        from that group's evaluation of 26 junior and senior
        high U.S. history textbooks published in 1986. The

panel rated the textbooks from good to exceptional in
quality, but expressed concern over excessive use of
readability formulas, uneven portrayal of women and
minority groups, a tendency to downplay conflict, and
inadequate treatment of religion.

361.   Lefever, E. W. (Ed.). (1978). Values in an American
          government textbook: three appraisals. Washington,
          D.C.: Ethics and Public Policy Center, Georgetown
          University.

        Presents assessments of American Government in
        Action (Charles E. Merrill, 1973) by three critics as
        part of the Center's project to "assess how well
        widely-used social science textbooks transmit the core
        values of our American heritage without short-changing
        American pluralism. (See items 340, 359, and 368.)

362.   Logan, W.C., & Needham, R.L. (1985). What elementary
          school social studies textbooks tell about the
          Vietnam War. The Social Studies, 76, 207-211.

        Presents the results of an analysis of 13 fifth-
        grade U.S. history textbooks using criteria based on a
        Nurse and Fleming study to determine the adequacy of
        the treatment of the Vietnam War. Found that all
        textbooks "presented too sketchy a picture to provide
        elementary students an adequate understanding of the
        Vietnam experience." Discusses some reasons for this
        state of affairs and suggests resources for teachers
        to use.

363.   McAulay, J.D. (1978). Evaluation of textbook content
          on Southeast Asia. The Clearing House, 52, 105-106.

        Summarizes the results of an evaluation by 14 gradu-
        ate students from Southeast Asia on the treatment of
        their countries in seven social studies textbooks used
        in the tenth grade. Most of the history of the area
        was treated very superficially and there were a number
        of serious omissions and distortions in the textbook
        presentation of the mores and customs of the people
        and the topography of the region. Suggests that more
        attention to the role of Southeastern nations in cur-
        rent affairs would be appropriate.

364.   McClure, D. (1952). Understanding about international
         agencies. Phi Delta Kappan, (Item 193), 292-294.

         Lists basic understandings suggested by authors of
         history texts, social psychologists, and authorities
         on international relations. Suggests that interna-
         tional agencies be so presented that students are
         helped to identify with the world community in which
         they live and with the other peoples of the world.

365.   Newitt, J. (1984). The pedagogy of fear and guilt: how
         textbooks treat the world economy. Social
         Education, 48, 47-48.

         Summarizes the results of a review of 63 high school
         history, civics, geography, and economics textbooks
         conducted for the Hudson Institute. Most textbooks
         employ the alienating image of a "widening gap" be-
         tween a few rich nations and a great mass of poor
         ones, ignoring the middle-income countries where life
         expectancy and GNP per capita increased between 1960
         and 1980, thus "substituting indoctrination for sub-
         stantive instruction."

366.   Patrick, J.J., & Hawke, S.D. (1982). Curriculum
         materials. In Morrisett, I. (Ed.). Social Studies
         in the 1980s. Washington, D.C.: Association for
         Supervision and Curriculum Development, 39-50.

         Summarizes findings of studies of textbook content
         published since 1975: "modeal social studies textbooks
         tend to be conventional" and emphasize the transmis-
         sion of information about "safe" topics. Concludes
         that "the best of the textbooks can be means to cer-
         tain objectives," such as acquisition of basic know-
         ledge, but other objectives, such as the learning of
         various attitudes, can best be met through the use of
         other educational media and practices.

367.   Ravitch, D. (1987). Tot sociology: or what happened to
         history in the grade schools? American Scholar, 56,
         343-354.

         Compares the "expanding environments" content of
         most current K-3 social studies programs with the
         study of mythology, legends, biographies, hero tales

and great events of Western literature and history
that made up the curriculum before the 1930s. Suggests that the earlier content be restored in the
interest of promoting "cultural literacy."

368.   Resnick, M., & Nerenberg, L.H., Response by the
        authors of American Government in Action. Values in
        an American government textbook (Item 361), 39-51.

        The authors defend their textbook on the basis of
        the audience for whom they were writing, the con-
        straints of publishing to a nationwide market, and
        other specific points of emphasis and interpretation
        on which they differ with their critics.

369.   Reyes, D.J. (1986). Critical thinking in elementary
        social studies text series. The Social Studies,
        77, 151-154.

        Identifies standards in the literature concerning
        the conceptualization and teaching of critical think-
        ing and compares treatments of critical thinking in
        five elementary social studies programs against these
        standards. Textbooks contain questions and unguided
        practice but do not provide systematic instruction or
        development of critical thinking, thinking, or reason-
        ing skills.

*   Reyes, D.J., & Smith, R.B. (1983). The role of concept
        learning in social studies textbook comprehension: a
        brief analysis. The Social Studies. (Cited above
        as Item 229.)

370.   Reynolds, C.J. (1952). Textbooks and immigrants. Phi
        Delta Kappan (Item 193), 295-296.

        Reports on a study of the treatment of immigrants in
        U.S. history textbooks published between 1861 and
        1947. Found different attitudes being transmitted
        during three periods: 1861-1891 basically "friendly";
        1891- 1930 mainly "critical"; 1930-1947 "sympathe-
        tic."

*   Rout, L. (1979). But out with the hippies! The Wall
        Street Journal. (Cited above as Item 148.

371.   Ryan, L. (1977). Judging textbooks: the Asia Society
        project. The Social Studies, 68, 236-240.

        Refers readers to the Asia Society Textbook evalua-
        tion project and suggests three questions textbook se-
        lection committees might ask: Who wrote the book?
        When was the book written? and What are the underlying
        assumptions about other cultures in the book? Gives
        examples of underlying assumptions found in secondary
        social studies textbooks.

372.   Schneider, D.O., & Van Sickle, R.L. (1979). The status
        of the social studies: the publishers' perspective.
        Social Education, 43, 461-465.

        Reports the results of a survey of 36 major publish-
        ers of social studies instructional materials to
        determine the degree of change and diversity in con-
        tent or instructional methodology. Found retrenchment
        from the dramatic changes of the 1960s and early
        1970s, due in large part to a general concern for
        basic education, but also a concern for the "humaniz-
        ing" of social studies.

373.   Social Education. (1986). Coming to grips with the
        great textbook machine. [Special section]. Social
        Education, 50, 39-70.

        Authors of the ten articles in this section examine
        the current national debate about social studies text-
        books -- what they should cover; what methods and
        techniques they should use; and what must occur if
        textbook quality is to improve.

        (Contains items, 080, 085, 116, 118, 158, 343, and
        380)

  *   Tyson-Bernstein, H., & Woodward, A. (1986). The great
        textbook machine and prospects for reform. Social
        Education (Item 085), 41-45.

374.   Wiley, K.B., & Race, J. (1977). Research on
        effectiveness and efficiency of social studies/
        social science educational materials. The status of
        pre-college science, mathematics, and social science
        education (Item 174), 194-196.

Summarizes five reviews of the literature that includes little research on effectiveness, except on
audiovisual, programmed, and "new social studies" materials.

375.   Wiley, K.B., & Race, J. (1977). The state of social
        studies curriculum materials. The status of pre-
        college science, mathematics, and social science
        education: 1955-1975, (Item 174), 80-119.

        Summarizes 161 content analysis studies of K-12
        textbooks and curriculum packages. Most-analyzed
        areas were social science content and methods, the
        treatment of specific themes, and the treatment of
        minorities.

376.   Wiley, M. (1982). Africa in social studies textbooks.
        Social Education, 46, 492-497, 548-552.

        Summarizes two earlier studies showing improvement
        in the treatment of Africa in more recent social stud-
        ies textbooks (see Item 382). Reports results of a
        more recent study of 13 secondary social studies text-
        books published between 1979 and 1981 that also found
        significant progress in the quantity of material about
        Africa, but points to remaining problems of over-
        emphasis on the lack of material achievements and
        hunting-gathering societies. There is also a failure
        to present the full range of African societies and the
        interdependence of African and other world economies.

377.   Wilson, A.H. (1980). The image of Africa in elementary
        schools. Social Education, 44, 503-507.

        Reports on an analysis of African content in 10
        basal readers. Found that folktales are favored over
        other literary forms and stories about animals over
        those with human characters. Concludes that there are
        too few stories about contemporary African children.
        Also reports on study of the effect of reading a real-
        istic story about modern African children on students
        in five sixth grade classrooms.

378.   Wilson, C.R., & Hammill, C. (1982). Inferencing and
        comprehension in ninth graders reading geography
        textbooks. Journal of Reading, 25, 424-428.

Gives results of a study in which poor, average, good, and superior readers were asked to say the information in a textbook passage in their own words. The good readers drew more inferences; poorer readers made a higher number of incorrect literal responses. Concludes that the poorer readers lacked appropriate background knowledge to understand the passage.

379.   Wojtan, L.S. (1981). Japan in our textbooks: the need for alternative resources. Georgia Social Science Journal, 12: 7-11.

Summarizes some preliminary findings of the Japan/ U.S. Textbook Study of secondary textbooks in U.S. history, geography, and world history, and grades 6-7 textbooks in world areas and cultures. Found selective and incomplete treatment of Japanese history, a misleading picture of modern Japan in geography textbooks, and an oversimplified view of Japan in the grade 6-7 texts. "Many easily rectified small errors abound in most of the books." Suggests that Japanese specialists should be consulted by textbook authors.

380.   Woodward, A., Elliott, D.L., & Nagel, K.C. (1986). Beyond textbooks in elementary social studies. Social Education (Item 373), 50-53.

Reports results of evaluations of ten social studies textbook programs. Found the programs to be of poor instructional quality because of a combination of factors: preoccupation with superficial yet broad content coverage, lack of care in content choice and presentation, absence of "point of view" and the use of readability formulas that result in "inconsiderate" content presentation.

381.   Zeikiros, A., & Wiley, M. (1977). Africa in Social Studies Textbooks. Madison: Wisconsin Department of Public Instruction.

Reports on problems found in a review of 55 social studies textbooks published in the 1960s and 1970s by curriculum specialists in African studies. These problems were found in the treatment of colonization and independence movements, climate and vegetation, wild animals, tribes and tribalism, emphasis on con-

flicts and political instability, and religions, among
others. Improved treatments were found in later editions when compared to earlier editions.

V.   IDEOLOGY AND CONTROVERSY

A. IDEOLOGY AND TEXTBOOK PROGRAMS

*   Anyon, J. (1979). Ideology and United States history textbooks. _Harvard Educational Review._ (Cited above as Item 335.)

382.   Belok, M. (1981). Schoolbooks, pedagogy books, and the political socialization of young Americans. _Educational Studies_, _12_(1), 35-41.

Reviews the influence of early educators on past schoolbooks and pedagogy books which served as vehicles for political socialization.

383.   DeCharms, R., & Moeller, G.H. (1962). Values expressed in American children's readers. _Journal of Abnormal and Social Psychology_, _64_(2), 136-142.

Investigates the incidence of achievement and affiliation imagery and moral teaching in a sample of children's readers from 1800 to the present.

*   Engle, S.H. (1986). Late night thoughts about the new social studies. _Social Education._ (Cited above as Item 158.)

*   Fleming, D. (1981). The impact of nationalism on world geography textbooks in the United States. _International Journal of Political Education._ (Cited above as Item 347.)

384.   Fratczak, B. (1981). School books as means of political socialization. _International Journal of Political Education_, _4_, 245-261.

Presents a comparative analysis of Polish primary-grade textbooks from two historical periods to determine the effect of the different political systems upon the politically-relevant content.

139

385.   Freebody, P., & Barker, C.D. (1985). Children's first
          schoolbooks: introductions to the culture of
          literacy. <u>Harvard Educational Review</u>, <u>55</u>, 381-398.

          Explores ways in which beginning readers serve as
          agents of socialization by presenting selected
          cultural perspectives to young children.

    *   Freeman, D.J., Kuhs, T.M., Porter, A.C., Floden, R.E.,
          Schmidt, W.H., & Schwille, J.H. (1983). Do textbooks
          and tests define a national curriculum in elementary
          mathematics? <u>The Elementary School Journal</u>. (Cited
          above as Item 266.)

    *   Gabler, M., & Gabler, N. (1982). Mind control through
          textbooks. <u>Phi Delta Kappan</u>. (Cited below as Item
          411.)

386.   Haavelsrud, M. (1980). Indoctrination or politiciza-
          tion through textbook content? <u>International
          Journal of Political Education</u>, <u>3</u>(1), 67-84.

          Summarizes findings of a study that explores the
          problem of indoctrinization and politicization in the
          content of civics textbooks approved for use in the
          Norwegian compulsory school.

    *   Hodenfield, G.K. (1979). U.S.-U.S.S.R Textbook
          Project. <u>American Education</u>. (Cited above as Item
          354.)

387.   Hurst, J.B. (1979). Political pablum: democratic role
          models in children's picture books. <u>Theory and
          Research in Social Education</u>, <u>7</u>(3), 1-19.

          Presents the results of a pilot study of a method
          for examining the "content" of children's books to
          determine the extent to which the major and secondary
          characters demonstrate active participation in
          politics and make realistic decisions.

    *   Jackson, P.W. (1983). The reform of science education:
          a cautionary tale. <u>Daedalus</u>. (Cited above as Item
          165.)

388.   Luke, C., DeCastell, S., & Luke, A. (1983). Beyond
        criticism: the authority of the school text.
        Curriculum Inquiry, 13, 111-127.

        Argues that the context of the curriculum in use
        reconstitutes the text, transforming it into other
        than its literal form.

389.   Page, A.L., & Clelland, D.A. (1978). The Kanawha
        County controversy: the authority of the school
        text. Social Forces, 57, 265-281.

        Analyzes the continuing protest over the content of
        textbooks used in the public schools of this West
        Virginia county within a reformulated theoretical
        framework of status politics derived from Weever and
        Gusfield. The background and development of the
        protest are examined as well as its organization,
        leadership, and basic issues.

*   Pearson, R.M. (1952). Can textbooks be subversive?
        Phi Delta Kappan. (Cited above as Item 143.)

*   Reynolds, J.C. (1981). Textbooks: guardians of
        nationalism. Education. (Cited above as Item
        195.)

*   Vitz, P. (1985). Textbook bias isn't of a
        fundamentalist nature. The Wall Street Journal.
        (Cited above as Item 197.)

390.   Walsted, W.R., & Watts, M.W. (1984). A response to
        Romanish: ideological bias in secondary economics
        textbooks. Theory and Research in Education, 11(4),
        25-35.

        Presents four main argument to refute the charges
        made by Romanish that recent economics textbooks
        contain ideological bias.

391.   Woodward, A. (1987). On teaching and textbook
        publishing: political issues obscure questions of
        pedagogy. Education Week, 6(17), 28, 22.

        Criticizes California's approach to textbook reform
        on the basis that it focuses on the presence and

absence of selected topics (some controversial) rather
than on the overall quality of instructional design as
a basis for rejecting textbooks.

392.   Zimet, S.F. (1969). American elementary reading text-
        books: a sociological review. The Teachers College
        Record, 70, 329-340.

Examines the content of reading texts as a) possible
contributing factors in reading retardation, and b)
transmitters of our cultural values and attitudes.
Striking differences were found between reading textbooks of the early colonial period and contemporary
basal readers, leading to a recommendation that
research findings be applied to textbook writing.

B. CONTROVERSY AND CENSORSHIP

393.   Arons, S. (1981). The crusade to ban books. Education
        Digest, 47(3), 2-5.

        Discusses the Pico case in terms of the First
        Amendment and the erosion of consensus about values.
        Argues that many groups feel their values are under
        attack and consequently are fighting back.

394.   Association for Supervision and Curriculum Develop-
        ment (1983). ASCD statement on censorship.
        Educational Leadership, 40, 54.

        Outlines six points on censorship covering profes-
        sional responsibility, selection of instructional
        materials, and the handling of complaints.

395.   Blume, J. (1982). What kids want to read. The
        National Elementary Principal, 61(3), 6-7.

        Notes that much censorship is caused by parental
        fear--fear of sexuality and reality. Urges teachers,
        administrators, librarians, and students to resist
        attempts to censor materials. Suggests that children
        are their own best censors and that they must have
        books that meet their own emotional needs.

396.   Bogert, E. (1985). Censorship and "The Lottery."
        English Journal, 74, 45-47.

        Discusses attempts to ban the story, The Lottery,
        and notes that, while it was not previously a target
        for censorship, the story challenges conservative
        traditions and thus has become a target for censor-
        ship.

397.   Brodinsky, B. (1982). The new right: the movement and
        its impact. Phi Delta Kappan, 64, 87-101.

Discusses the danger to public education of attacks from the New Right, which is characterized as an "aberrant conservative movement" consisting of both concerned parents and "zealots and extremists," with the goals of eliminating the separation between church and state and creating competing education institutions that will bleed public schools of support. (See also 405, 411, 426, 437, and 439.)

398.   Burress, L., & Jenkins, E.B. (1982). The student's right to know. Urbana, IL: National Council of Teachers of English.

The fundamental tenet of education is the student's right to know—that is derived from the teacher's right to teach. Both of these rights must be safeguarded, while acknowledging parental values and concerns and taking appropriate action. Describes procedures for dealing with complaints about instructional materials.

399.   Cawelti, G., & Olson, N.S. (1982). Limiting what students shall read. The National Elementary Principal, 61(3). 12-14.

Presents a report of the ASCD/ALA survey that found increasing attempts to censor school materials. Makes recommendations concerning selection policies, procedures for reviewing complaints and the like.

400.   Ciolli, R. (1983). The textbook wars. The Newsday Magazine (December 13). 11, 23, 26, 28.

Describes how various special interest groups attempt to influence textbook content in Texas. The effect on the rest of the country, publishers, and textbooks are detailed.

401.   Clark, E. (1986). A slow, subtle exercise in censorship. School Library Journal, 32(7), 93-96.

A district librarian describes a decision by the Hanover School Board to institute a parental permission policy for students who wanted to borrow books by Judy Blume.

402.   Cohen, B. (1986). Censoring the sources. <u>School
         Library Journal</u>, <u>32</u>(7), 97-99.

         Describes how Harcourt Brace Jovanovich wanted per-
         mission to include a well-known author's children's
         story in a new reading basal but wanted to eliminate
         mention of Jews, the Jewish holiday Sukkos, God, and
         the Bible because of concern over potential contro-
         versy.

403.   Considine, D.M. (1985). Censorship, the classroom, and
         the electronic environment. <u>English Journal</u>, <u>74</u>,
         38-41.

         Argues that attempts to "protect" the young through
         censorship are ineffective, given the broad access
         everyone has to the "electronic environment." Suggests
         that the young should instead be helped to become
         critical consumers of materials who are able to
         recognize those that are manipulative or debasing.

  *   Dahlin, R. (1981). A tough time for textbooks.
         <u>Publishers Weekly</u>. (Cited above as Item 105.)

404.   Dick, J. (1982). North of 49: schools and
         controversial books in Canada. <u>Phi Delta Kappan</u>,
         <u>63</u>, 448-449.

         Argues that a growing conservatism and a retreat
         from "compromise" and flexibility have resulted in an
         increase in censorship attempts. Describes the cen-
         sorship activities of various groups such as "Renais-
         sance Canada."

405.   Dixon, G. (1982). The deliberate sabotage of education
         by liberal elitists. <u>Phi Delta Kappan</u>, <u>64</u>, 97.

         Argues that those in control of public education are
         out of touch with public sentiment and that the public
         schools should return to basic instruction. (See also
         Item 397).

406.   Donelson, K. (1985). Almost 13 years of book protests:
         now what? <u>School Library Journal</u>, <u>31</u>(7), 93-98.

Presents a compilation of surveys and reports on censorship incidents and the books most frequently protested.

407.   Donelson, K. (1983). Giving comfort to the enemy: how teachers and librarians aid the censor. The High School Journal, 66, 155-161.

Asserts that censorship is an age-old phenomenon in which teachers and librarians have never been active participants. Identifies three kinds of teacher/ librarian censor: moral, literary, and sociological. Suggests that educating teachers and librarians to fight against censorship should have high priority.

408.   Doyle, D.P. (1982). Censorship and the challenge to intellectual freedom. The National Elementary Principal, 61(3), 8-11.

Describes a number of censorship attempts, especially those attributed to the Gablers and such organizations as the Moral Majority. Argues that many parents, students, librarians, and teachers are using notions of "intellectual freedom" and freedom of expression to counter these censorship attempts.

409.   Fitzgerald, F. (1984). A Reporter at Large: a dis- agreement in Baileyville. The New Yorker (January 16), 47-90.

Presents an extensive analysis of a censorship incident in Baileyville, Maine, in which the values and motives of all parties--school adminstrators, school board members, the protesting parents and their supporting church, and other community members are dissected and described. The tension between the values of the various groups and the socialization function of the school are highlighted and the inci- dent discussed in light of recent Supreme Court deci- sions.

410.   Foley, R. (1982). The community's role in dealing with censorship. Educational Leadership, 40, 51-55.

Discusses the reasons for a common adversarial rela- tionship between school and community over selection

of library books and instructional materials--e.g.,
educator unwillingness "to accept the possibility that
the community has a legitimate role" in such selection under the aegis of intellectual freedom. Suggests an alternative method for dealing with censorship on the basis of due process. Lists 10 guidelines
for dealing with citizen challenges to school books
and materials.

*   Frymier, J. (1983). A tribute to publishers.
          Education Forum. (Cited above as Item 114.)

411.   Gabler, M., & Gabler, N. (1982). Mind control through
          textbooks. Phi Delta Kappan, 64, 96.

          Argues that educators are out of touch with the
          values of society and that textbooks reflect the bias
          of a liberal view of education and society. (See also
          Item 397.)

412.   Glenn, C.L. (1987). Textbook controversies: a
          "disaster for public schools"? Phi Delta Kappan,
          68, 451-455.

          Argues for a creative response to the Mozert v.
          Hawkins County Public Schools ruling that certain
          textbooks violate religious beliefs. Suggests that
          educators need to listen sympathetically to the
          concerns of conservative Christian parents.

413.   Hefley, J.C. (1979). Are textbooks harming your
          children? Milford, MI: Mott Media.

          Tells the story of how Norma and Mel Gabler became
          nationally prominant critics of textbooks and how they
          successfully challenged textbooks submitted for adop-
          tion in Texas, charging that they had unpatriotic con-
          tent, included evolution and excluded creationism, and
          downplayed basic American family values. Details
          presentations to the Texas adoption committee
          and reprints Gabler reviews of a number of text-
          books.

414.   Holden, C. (1987). Textbook controversy intensifies
          nationwide. Science, 235, 19-21.

Discusses recent Supreme Court cases and attempts at
censorship, noting that they reflect a broader socie-
tal conflict over values. Observes that publisher
attempts to deal with these conflicts result in bland
and uniform textbooks. Quotes several authorities in
arguing for a more responsive and hence a more regional textbook industry.

416.   Hulsizer, D. (1987). Public education on trial.
        Educational Leadership, 44, 12-16.

Describes recent court challenges to textbook
content in Alabama and Tennessee and discusses the
effects of these cases on classrooms, teachers, and
the purpose of public education. (See also Item 432.)

417.   Jenkinson, E.B. (1985). Protecting Holden Caufield and
        his friends from the censors. English Journal, 74,
        26-33.

Presents a general discussion of trends in censorship and describes the activities of various special
interest groups. Suggest ten steps teachers should
take to ensure books are not censored.

418.   Jenkinson, E.B. (1983). The tale of Tell City: an
        anti-censorship saga. Washington, D.C.: People for
        the American Way.

Presents a case study of a censorship attempt in
Tell City, Indiana. Following a ninth grader's com-
plaint about Of Mice and Men, a group led by a minis-
ter demanded the removal of books, and protests then
escalated. Describes how the rest of the community,
the school board, and teachers "fought back," refuting
the protesters' charges and stating the intention to
defend "the Constitutional right of individuals."

419.   Jenkinson, E.B. (1983). Censors in the classroom.
        Carbondale: Southern Illinois University Press.

Traces the growth of censorship attempts and describes cases east and west of the Mississippi, the
Kanawha County controversy, censorship organizations,
and other topics.

419.   Kamhi, M.M. (1982). Censorship vs. selection: choosing
        books for schools. American Education, 18(2),
        11-16.

        Gives results of a large-scale study of censorship
        attempts based on responses from librarians and school
        principals. Found that censorship attempts increased
        between 1976 and 1980. These attempts were initiated
        at the state level usually by organized groups
        concerned with broad issues of content, curriculum,
        and ideology. At the local level, the attempts were
        usually initiated by individuals concerned with issues
        of sexuality and profanity. Notes the importance of
        having established policies and procedures for dealing
        with censorship.

420.   Kelly, M.G., & Gross, R.E. (1981). Controversy and
        social studies textbooks: a model code. The Social
        Studies, 72, 61-64.

        Suggests that one way to stem criticism of the
        coverage of controversial issues is to accept a "fair-
        ness doctrine," similar to that accepted by broad-
        casters, requiring any controversial issue to receive
        a balanced presentation.

421.   Kline, M.R. (1984). Social influences in textbook
        publishing. The Educational Forum, 48, 223-234.

        Presents a historical study tracing censorship
        attempts on instructional materials, including efforts
        by the Ku Klux Klan, the Daughters of the American
        Revolution, civil rights activists, feminists, and
        others.

422.   Lehr, F. (1985). Academic freedom: a guide to major
        court cases. English Journal, 74, 42-44.

        Reviews documents in the ERIC system that cover
        major court decisions dealing with academic freedom.

423.   Lewis, J.B. (1980). Freedom of speech and expression
        in the public schools: a closer look at teacher's
        rights. High School Journal, 63, 137-145.

        Reviews legal precedents on freedom of speech and
        expression, especially as it relates to teachers.

424.   Massie, D.C. (1984). Censorship and the question of
        balance. Social Education, 48, 145-147.

        Discusses the argument that right wing efforts to
        ban books and the left's attempts to ban materials
        offensive to minorities are both forms of censorship.
        Analyzes the motives of the actors in terms of the
        objects, aims, and consequences of protest and finds
        right wing extremists wish to restrict discussion and
        ideas while the left deals with socially accepted
        goals.

425.   McGraw, O. (1982). Censorship and the public schools:
        who decides what students will read? American
        Education, 18(10), 8-14.

        Locates the problem of censorship in the clash of
        values between parents (and community) and educators.
        Holds that educators often ignore the values of par-
        ents, invoking professional judgment and academic
        freedom as reasons for adopting and using controver-
        sial materials.

426.   McGraw, O. (1982). Where is the public in public
        education? Phi Delta Kappan, 64, 94-95.

        Argues that the widespread criticism of, and
        dissatisfaction with education is caused by the lack
        of responsiveness on the part of educators and others
        to the demands of parents. (See also Item 397.)

427.   National Council of Teachers of English (1982). State-
        ment of censorship and professional guidelines.
        Urbana, IL: Author.

        Presents an official statement distinguishing
        between censorship and professional guidelines.
        Offers practical suggestions for writing professional
        guidelines and selecting instructional materials.

428.   Nocera, J. (1982). The big book-banning brawl. The
        New Republic, (September 13), 20-24.

        Holds that there is a built-in tension between

liberty and authority in the public schools and argues
that the judgment of the librarian should not always
be considered sacred and that the values of parents
and the needs of young people should also be
considered.

*   Page, A.L., & Clelland, D.A. (1978). The Kanawha
       County controversy: the authority of school text.
       Social Forces. (Cited above as Item 389.)

429.   Parker, B., & Weiss, S. (1983). Protecting the freedom
       to learn. Washington, D.C.: People for the American
       Way.

       Describes the major organizations involved in
censorship attempts and the "anti-public education
movement." Offers suggestions for how groups can
organize to prevent censorship. Appendixes contain
numerous reprints of relevant articles and reports.

430.   Raywid, M.A. (1979). Censorship: new wrinkles in an
       old problem. High School Journal, 62, 332-338.

       Uses examples from "left" and "right" to show how,
although censorship is often seen as a "black and
white" issue, it is difficult to arrive at objective
decisions about what and what not to censor.

431.   Richardson, E.H. (1979). Textbook censorship and
       intolerance in the classroom. Drexel Library
       Quarterly, 18(1), 82-94.

       Explains the surge in censorship attempts in terms
of the on-going attack on middle class values as a
result of which the middle class feels isolated and
threatened. Notes that it is no longer possible to
tolerate censorship, given our pluralistic society.

432.   Rowell, C.G. (1987). Implications of the Tennessee
       textbook controversy for public education.
       Educational Leadership, 44), 14-15.

       Lists eight implications of the Mozert et al. v.
Hawkins County Public Schools et al. ruling that are
cause for concern among public school officials and
parents "who view public education in a broader

context than do (the) plaintiffs." (See also Item
416.)

433.   Ryan, J., Huey-Stone, B., Lovejoy, S.C., Kaskey, S.,
Witcher, S., Swetnam, M.I., & McKenzie, M. (1983).
Pico v. Board of Education, Island Trees Union Free
School District No. 26: an analysis. In Aaron,
S.L., & Scales, P.R. (Eds.). School Library Media
Annual. Littleton, CO: Libraries Unlimited. 33-42.

Describes the banning of such books as Slaughter-
house-Five and The Naked Ape by order of the Island
Trees School District Board. Analyzes the litigation
and the 1982 Supreme Court ruling and draws implications.

434.   Schipper, M.C. (1983). Textbook controversy: past and
present. New York University Education Quarterly,
14(3-4), 31-36.

Describes the 1939-1942 efforts to ban the Harold
Rugg junior high textbook series called Man and His
Changing Society. Covers the development of the
series, the attackers, and the defenders and draws
implications for our understanding of current attacks
on textbooks and literature for young people.

*   Schomburg, C. (1986). Texas and social studies texts.
Social Education. (Cited above as Item 080.)

435.   Seiferth, B.B. (1982). A cloud of censorship over
secondary schools. High School Journal, 65,
151-156.

Presents a detailed discussion of censorship in
Illinois based on a survey of 200 high school princi-
pals.

436.   Simmons, J.S. (1981). Proactive censorship: the new
wave. English Journal, 70, 18-20.

Asserts that textbook authors engage in self-
censorship because of the sensitivity of publishers to
state and local textbook requirements and the lobbying
of both right and left for the exclusion and inclusion
of certain content.

437.   Stahlschmidt, A. (1982). A workable strategy for
        dealing with censorship. Phi Delta Kappan, 64,
        99-101.

        Gives a detailed report on how one school district
        deals with challenges to instructional materials,
        including statistics on the number of challenges.
        (See also Item 397.)

438.   Stanek, L.W. (1985). Huck Finn: 100 years of durn fool
        problems. School Library Journal, 31(6), 19-22.

        Notes that in its centennial year, Huckleberry Finn
        is as controversial as when it was first published.

439.   Stein, J.A. (1982). No real solutions to a very real
        problem. Phi Delta Kappan, 64, 98.

        Holds that the attacks on education by the New Right
        jeopardizes America's pluralistic approach to educa-
        tion and that these attacks should be resisted. How-
        ever, educators must recognize deficiencies in school
        and respond to them. (See also Item 397.)

440.   Stern, N. (1979). Challenging ideological exclusion of
        curriculum material: rights of students and parents.
        Harvard Civil Rights-Civil Liberties Law Review, 14,
        485-528.

        Discusses the rejection of the state history text-
        book, Mississippi: Conflict and Change, by the state
        board of education in light of attempts to impose
        ideological criteria on the selection of textbooks.
        Argues that school boards do not have unrestricted
        authority to exclude materials based on ideological
        content and describes the constitutional rights of
        students and parents in challenging such decisions.

441.   Vitz, P. (1986). Censorship: evidence of bias in our
        children's textbooks. Ann Arbor, MI: Servant Books.

        Reports findings of a study of basal readers and
        U.S. history textbooks that reveal an absence of
        patriotism and religion in contemporary American life
        and in American history. The study also found dis-
        torted presentations of family life.

442.   Watras, J. (1983). Problems in multi-cultural
        education: the textbook controversy in Kanawha
        County, West Virginia. Journal of Curriculum
        Theorizing. 5(1), 4-16.

        Analyzes the Kanawha County textbook controversy and
        criticizes previous analyses for considering the con-
        troversy only in terms of cultural conflict.

443.   Worthington, P. (1986). Writing a rationale for a
        controversial common reading book: Alice Walker's
        The Color Purple. English Journal, 74, 48-52.

        Suggests that teachers should write rationales for
        using potentially controversial books. Identifies
        points of controversy (subject matter, words, gram-
        mar), using The Color Purple as an example, and sug-
        gests responses to them.

444.   Wynne, E.A. (1985). The case for censorship to protect
        the young. Issues in Education, 3(3), 171-184.

        Argues that the traditional definition of censorship
        has expanded to include the right of children and
        adolescents to receive information. Argues that this
        expanded definition ignores the need to protect young
        people from the tensions and problems of adulthood,
        noting that adults can make good judgments regarding
        what is appropriate for the young.

C. EVOLUTION AND CREATIONISM

445.   Christy, O.B. (1937). The development of the teaching
        of general biology in the secondary schools
        [Monograph]. Journal of the Tennessee Academy of
        Science, 12, 293-341.

        Gives results of a study tracing the treatment of
        evolution in textbooks between the 1880s and the
        1930s. Found that evolution was always a controver-
        sial topic that was given only minor coverage in text-
        books and the agitation against the teaching of evolu-
        tion in the 1920s resulted in even less coverage.

446.   Down from the apes (1985). The Economist (September
        21), 26-27.

        Reports on the decision of the California State
        Board of Education to reject all science textbooks
        submitted for adoption for their failure to adequately
        cover controversial subjects such as evolution,
        ethics, and human reproduction.

447.   Ellis, W.E. (1983). Biology teachers and border state
        beliefs. Society, 20(2), 26-30.

        Gives results of a survey of high school biology
        teachers in Kentucky, Indiana, and Tennessee to
        determine the relative emphasis given to evolution in
        their teaching. Those reporting no/little emphasis:
        23%-40%; moderate/strong emphasis: 43%-77%. How
        evolution was treated in the textbooks influenced
        teachers' responses to the survey questions.

448.   Grabiner, J.V., & Miller, P.D. (1974). Effects of the
        Scopes trial. Science, 185, 832-837.

        Reports on a historical study of the treatment of
        evolution in textbooks published between 1900 and
        1964. Notes that the Scopes trial resulted in less

coverage and coverage was often eliminated or placed
at the end of the text. With the publication of BSCS
materials in the 1960s, evolution received full coverage again.

449.   Hellmann, R.A. (1985). Evolution in American school
        biology books from the late 19th century until the
        1930s. American Biology Teacher, 47, 778-780.

        Examines the treatment of evolution in biology texts
        between 1880 and the 1930s. Found that evolution was
        gradually included in textbooks and that by 1926 "con-
        tinued to provide a mainstream of thought in text-
        books."

450.   Knight, J. (1985). Creation--science, evolution--
        science and education: anything goes? Australian
        Journal of Education, 29, 115-132.

        Discusses the debate over evolution and creationism
        in Queensland, Australia and the United States.
        Examines evolution and creationism drawing on theories
        and philosophies of science. Concludes that creation
        science does not meet the criteria for being a
        science and that creationist protest reflects "human
        alienation" and dissatisfaction with modern society.

451.   Laba, E.R., & Gross, E.W. (1955). Evolution slighted
        in high school biology. The Clearinghouse, 24,
        396-399.

        Reports on a survey of Essex County, New Jersey
        teacher attitudes toward the treatment of evolution.
        Teachers reported that several books did not mention
        "evolution" and that, in general, coverage was mini-
        mal. Nine of the teachers believed in supernatural
        causes of organic change.

452.   Le Clerq, F.S. (1974). The Constitution and
        creationism. American Biology Teacher, 36, 139-145.

        Analyzes the creationism controversy in light of
        Constitutional law and recent court cases.

453.   Lewin, R. (1984). Antievolution rules are unconstitu-
         tional. Science, 223, 1373-1374.

         Reports on the State Attorney General's ruling
         striking down the Texas State Board of Education
         policy that textbooks should treat evolution as a
         theory and not a fact. Argues that the policy had
         resulted in a substantial reduction in the coverage of
         evolution.

454.   Maeroff, G.I. (1982). Survival of the fittest and
         educational publishing. Curriculum Review, 21,
         429/S1-430/S2.

         Describes the rejection of three high school biology
         textbooks by New York City for their inadequate treat-
         ment of evolution.

455.   McDaniel, G.I. (1983). Creation and evolution:
         questions and quandries. The Educational Forum, 48,
         115-122.

         Concludes, after reviewing 50 years of the evolu-
         tion/creationism controversy, that there are certain
         well established principles concerning evolution and
         the role of educators. Notes that evolution is a
         scientific theory and science cannot be excluded from
         the curriculum and that, although government must
         remain neutral in matters of religion, evolution is
         not a religious doctrine.

456.   Moore, T.R. (1983). Creationism in California.
         Daedalus, 103, 173-189.

         Gives a detailed description of the successful
         efforts of creationists to change the California state
         framework for science such that the inclusion of
         creationism as an alternative "theory" to evolution is
         mandated in biology textbooks. Discusses the efforts
         by educators and scientists to overturn the decision.

457.   Moyer, W.A. (1985). How Texas rewrote your textbooks.
         The Science Teacher, 52, 23-27.

         Shows how, because it spends millions of dollars on
         textbooks, Texas exerts great influence on the kinds

of textbooks publishers produce. For example, due to
the influence of Texas-based special interest groups,
there has been a decline in the coverage of evolution
in science textbooks.

458.   Nelkin, D. (1982). The creation controversy: science
          or scripture in the schools. New York: Norton.

          Describes the efforts of special interest groups
          from the 1920s to the present to ban the teaching of
          the theory of evolution or to ensure "equal time" for
          the teaching of creationism. Also covers the often
          successful attempt to ban the innovative Man: A Course
          of Study elementary school curriculum materials.
          Discusses the social and cultural reasons for anti-
          science activities.

459.   Nelkin, D. (1983). Legislating creation in Arkansas.
          Society, 20, 13-16.

          Discusses in detail the successful efforts of
          Arkansas creationists to obtain a statute requiring
          "equal time" for creationism in the school curriculum
          and the subsequent court case overturning that
          statute. (See also 461.)

460.   Novak, M. (1983). False foes. Society, 20, 31-35.

          Argues that creationism has become a powerful symbol
          of the fallibility of science and the fractured cul-
          ture and values of society.

461.   Overton, W.R. (1983). The decision on McLean v.
          Arkansas Board of Education. Society, 20, 3-12.

          Gives the full text of U.S. District Judge Overton's
          decision overturning the Arkansa statute mandating
          "equal time" for the teaching of the theory of evolu-
          tion and creationism. [See also 459.]

462.   Pearson, C. (1981). Can teachers cope with
          creationism? Learning, 9(7), 31-33.

          Argues that textbooks tend to give an inaccurate
          account of evolution, glossing over the gaps and the
          questions that scientists are currently exploring.

Suggests that teachers need to have more than a textbook knowledge of evolution so they can deal with the
dogmatism of creationism.

463.   Rosenthal, D.B. (1985). Evolution in high school
        biology textbooks. Science Education, 69, 637-648.

        Presents results of an analysis of 22 high school
        biology textbooks published between 1963 and 1983 that
        showed a decline in content devoted to evolution.
        Judged the treatment of evolution in these textbooks
        ranged from "fair" to "excellent."

464.   Saladin, K.S. (1983). Sixty years of creationism in
        Georgia. Society, 20, 17-25.

        Gives a history of the attempts to censor the teach-
        ing of evolution in Georgia schools, together with an
        overview of recent activities of creationism
        supporters.

465.   Skoog, G. (1984). The coverage of evolution in high
        school biology textbooks published in the 1980s.
        Science Education, 68, 117-128.

        Presents the results of an analysis of six high
        school biology textbooks, first published in the
        1970s, indicating that the coverage of evolution
        declined in four and remained the same in two. Five
        textbooks published for the first time in the 1980s
        were found to cover evolution less extensively than
        the previously published volumes.

466.   Skoog, G. (1984). Topic of evolution in secondary
        school biology textbooks: 1900-1977. Science
        Education, 63, 621-640.

        Combines the results of a previous study of 83
        textbooks published between 1900 and 1969 with an
        analysis of ten textbooks published between 1970 and
        1977. Found that, prior to 1960, evolution was
        cursorily covered, that the publication of the BSCS
        materials reversed this trend, but that textbooks
        published in the 1970s again reflected a reluctance to
        fully include evolution.

467.   Troost, C.J. (1968). Evolution in biological education
        prior to 1960. Science Education, 50, 300-301.

        Gives a historical study of evolution in textbooks
        from the 1800s to 1960.

468.   Wade, B. (1972). Creationists and evolutionists:
        confrontation in California. Science, 178, 724-729.

        Discusses the decision by the California State Board
        of Education to require that textbooks include crea-
        tionist explanations of development. Details the role
        of the Creation Research Society in persuading the
        Board to adopt this policy and the responses of scien-
        tists.

469.   Williams, M.B. (1985) The scientific status of
        evolutionary theory. The American Biology Teacher,
        47, 205-210.

        Argues that evolutionary theory, based on certain
        tests and principles, is a legitimate scientific
        theory.

470.   Woodward, A., & Elliott, D.L. (1987). Evolution and
        creationism in high school textbooks. The American
        Biology Teacher, 49, 164-169.

        Reports the results of an analysis of 15 high school
        biology textbooks published between 1977 and 1983.
        The textbooks were found to fall in four categories in
        their treatment of evolution: a) those that totally
        avoided evolution and Darwin, b) those taking a
        "balanced" approach by including both evolution and
        creationism, c) those excluding human evolution, and
        d) those (like the BSCS volumes) giving evolution full
        and extensive coverage.

*   Woodward, A. (1987). On teaching and textbook publish-
        ing: political issues obscure questions of pedagogy.
        Education Week. (Cited above as Item 391.)

471.   Zuidema, H.P. (1981). Less evolution, more creationism
        in textbooks. <u>Educational Leadership</u>, <u>39</u>, 217-218.

        Discusses the effect creationist special interest
        groups have had on publishers. Notes that publishers
        have responded to "the market" by producing textbooks
        that give less coverage to evolution than before.

Agostino, V.R., 333

American Textbook Publishers Institute, 034, 090

Ames, S.A., 207

Ames, W.S., 202

Anderson, C.W., 273

Anderson, L., 274

Anderson, N., 334

Anderson, R.C., 169, 275

Anderson, T.H., 204, 222, 276

Anyon, J., 335

Apple, M.W., 091

Archibald, G., 092

Armbruster, B.B., 203, 204, 205, 222, 276, 277

Arnold, L., 241

Arons, S., 393

Association for Supervision and Curriculum Development, 394

Aukerman, R.C., 286

Babikian, E., 308

Bagley, W.C., 001

Bailey, M.H., 302

Ballenger, M., 262

Barger, H.M., 336

Barker, C.D., 385

Barrass, R., 309

Barone, W.P., 333

Baskin, B., 242

Baumann, J.F., 206

Beattie, C., 028

Beck, I.L., 002, 279, 280

Beck, R., 334

Becker, J., 337

Becker, J.M., 351

Belli, G.M., 267

Belok, M., 382

Benham, N. 262

Bernstein, H. (See Tyson-Bernstein)

Bierstedt, R., 093

Birchall, G., 338

Black, H., 094

Blankenship, G., 249

Blosser, P.E., 318

Blume, J., 395

Bogert, E., 396

Bohning, G., 281

Boller, P.F., Jr., 098

Bond, G.L., 282

Bordelon, K.W., 243

Bowler, M., 029, 095, 096, 097

Bradley, J.M., 202, 217

Bragdon, H.W., 099, 100

Brammer, M., 101

Broadnax,, W.D., 329

Brodinsky, B., 397

Brody, P.J., 310

Broudy, E., 102

Brown, E., 103

Bruce, B., 283

Burress, L., 398

Burton, W.H., 176

Butterfield, R.A., 244

Bybee, R.W., 319

Cahen, L.S., 003

Callahan, L.G., 263

Carrick, T., 311

Carroll, J.D., 339

Cawelti, G., 399

Chall, J.S., 177, 210, 284, 285

Chambers, F. 208

163

SUBJECT INDEX